Never Gave Up

An Émigré Story

Life, Migration and Struggles of a Resilient Iranian Woman

By Farah Farnia

"There was one; there was no one; other than God there was no one."

1st English Edition

With Additions to Farsi Edition

Cover Design: Amin Ashkan and O. Allen

Translation & Edit: O. Allen

ISBN: 9798721976162

Acknowledgements

I am pleased to thank all the family members and friends who took part in helping and encouraging me to write my life story.

I am especially indebted to,

Dr. Minoo Varzegar, for encouragingly standing by my side throughout this journey.

Dr. Maaboud Ansari, for his review and critique of my book.

Dr. Minoo Gorji, for graciously lending her sound advice and keen observations.

Dr. Shahlah Abghari, for her insightful review of this work.

My faithful daughter, Setareh, for bolstering me with her presence, support, and unmatched encouragement as my life bent with twists and turns.

My caring nephew, Fardad, to whom I am especially indebted for his indispensable assistance related to financial matters in Iran, including those related to my tenure at the Ministry of Health.

My grandson Bahador, who edited and prepared my book for publication.

O. Allen, who spared no efforts in translating my book into a lucid English narrative, in the best possible manner, I am especially grateful.

A Word with the Reader

"I was on that day when the Names were not, nor any sign of existence endowed with name, by me Names and Named were brought to view, on the day when there was not 'I' and 'We'...,"

~ Rumi

"Of migration..., in which the past becomes dreamy because its symbols have all vanished, and the present too is dreamy because it is linked with no memories...,"

~ George Eliot

Those who migrate from their lands face obstacles, such as cultural, financial, homesickness, and the like. Rough patches, they pass, before the idiosyncratic culture, peculiar to the new land, sinks in by degrees. Immigration to the land of the free was especially difficult in 1978 when America would not open its arms to us Iranians, and I was no exception.

But I chose to brace myself to overcome all that stood on my path, endured hardships aplenty with an abiding faith and a resolute spirit, and never gave up.

This work is an attempt to recount an émigré's ups & downs, and the struggles they beget. I have tried to, herein, with an objective eye on the past, tell a story of how and why I was propelled to undertake this perilous journey that I survived in the end. I have also tried to remember the dear ones who traveled this fateful path together with me.

It is with the hope that this account will be of some use to those who have walked this path, those who are walking this path, or those who will be walking this path.

Table of Contents

Preface

*"The wind bloweth where it listeth, & thou hearest
the sound thereof, but canst not tell whence it
cometh, & whither it goeth: so is every one that is
born of the Spirit...,"*

~ *John 3:8, KJV*

*"... writing is always a breaking of the soil, clearing
away prejudices, pulling up of sour weeds of crooked
thinking, stripping the turf so as to get at what is
fertile beneath...,"*

~ *Henry Seidel Canby*

The sky is laden with a thick dark cloud, ominously covering all that the eye can see, seeping its gloom into the room. My world is hung on its orbit in suspension. Time has come to a halt. A deep, creeping silence has overcome the discernible world. I am lost in thought, musing, casting my vacant gaze through the window on the hazy horizon; forlorn and sad...

"Whence cometh this heavy sorrow?" I ask myself.

I search for the marrow of my pain. The indelible, distant life I have lived passes through my memory in a throng of scenes, connected, disjointed, and connected again, in tandem, like a motion picture. A labyrinth of perplexities and countless questions left unanswered, form in my mind.

Bitter and sweet reminiscences of my age of innocence and naiveté; injustices endured, and the inability to defend myself, haunt me. I wistfully wonder,

"What was it that suddenly rose in me? What was it that bolstered me and saved me from succumbing to my surroundings? Why did I suddenly

7

choose action over acquiescence?"

I rose and with intrepid courage said,

"I am."

Yes, I rose, took the high road, and claimed my life. Yes, I grew stronger in the face of adversity, honed with each set-back, like a diamond, and I stood my ground. Yes, indeed.

Suddenly, all eyes turned upon me. I tried with tooth and nail to make my family happy, gave all to them, and enjoyed it too. I endured the painful loss of dear ones, had numerous brushes of my own with death, journeyed through life's rough patches, rolled with the ebbs and the flows, but survived in the end with patience and perseverance.

I survived because I believe I was destined to play a larger role in life, a Platonic role perhaps. I survived to help and assist my family and others who needed me. I became a liaison, a conduit, a catalyst, helping family and friends, including my loins, to migrate to America, the land of the free, the home of the brave, in search of a better life.

Migration to America, this unfathomable land, marked a tumultuous chapter in my life. The odds were stacked high against me. I had studied interior design but could not land a job in that field in America because I had no experience and could barely speak English. I also lacked sufficient capital to freely risk venturing out on my own.

But I was ebullient. I was effervescent with hope, passion, self-confidence, and resilience, which enabled me to build, anew, a better life. During the past 40 years that I have lived in America, I have either started or have been involved in businesses in as many as eight different fields as diverse as hospitality, retail, and real estate. On top of all that, I have been able to obtain both a travel agency license and a real estate license. I have been able to overcome hurdle after hurdle. And whenever I failed, I rose to my feet and tried again.

The last venture I initiated was a quick-service restaurant franchise. I had expected, as stipulated in our contract, to receive the bare, essential support from the franchisor, needed to succeed. I had planned to retire after this last venture. But it did not happen as I had hoped. Although the "due diligence" I undertook to ensure the viability of this venture was not short of extensive, the franchisor turned out to be a sham. I soon realized that the franchisor was only interested in unloading his equipment and products on me, not much more, and ended up failing me on his pledge of support.

No matter how hard I tried, the business did not make it. It exhausted all of my financial resources. In addition to all of my savings, it dried up all of my credit facilities. It eventually pushed me into involuntary bankruptcy, an arena until then unbeknown to me, causing me to, on top of tarnishing my impeccable credit, which I had painstakingly maintained through thick and thin of my active life, lose all I had worked for and saved. While this blow struck me at an old age, it too, either physically or emotionally, failed to affect me. It, too, failed to shake me. It, too, failed to deter me.

Neither did I lose hope, nor passion, to continue living a sanguine life.

Perhaps, it has been my abiding faith that has sustained me time and again; faith in destiny; faith in my maker, the almighty, the absolute, as all else is nothing but relative.

I continue to enjoy the success of my loved ones with ever more zest, and as before, I devour life with insatiable passion. Deep in rumination, I suddenly lose the train of my thoughts with the phone ringing. I answer,

"Hello, Pooneh?"

"Hi Auntie, how're you? How's everything?"

"Oh, I guess I'm OK, Dearie. How about you?"

"I'm just fine. But you don't sound too well."

"How did you guess?"

"I can tell by the tone of your voice. Tell me, what's wrong?"

"Oh, nothing. I'm just a little sad today. I've been thinking about the past. The weather here is dreary today, and bittersweet memories have been popping up in my mind all day."

"It's normally like that when it's cloudy and grim. But come to think of it, have you ever thought of writing these memories of yours...maybe even into a book?"

"What...A book?"

"Yeah, why not? So far as I can remember you've done plenty in your lifetime. Others can always learn from your experiences. Yeah, you should. You should write a book. Next time I call you, I want you to read me your life story. I wanna make sure you've started writing! A book, that is!"

Pooneh and I have a close relationship. She often asks me for advice about general matters, particularly business. She also asks me about matters of faith and eschatology. Like my daughter, Setareh, she has always been a rock in my life.

Lo and behold, with Pooneh's wild suggestion and her continued reminders, instead of brooding over my past, I began to write down my memoirs. I began to write from time immemorial, when I was nearly four years old, to the present.

Blackstone Bazaar, Shiraz

"There are two important days in your life, first is the day you're born, second is the day you know why you were born..."

~ *Mark Twain*

Shiraz, one of the oldest cities of ancient Persia, its origins dating back to 2,000 B.C., a trade center for over a thousand years, is located on the Rudkhaneye Khoshk (The Dry River), in the southwest plain of Iran. The city was restored under Umayyads in the 7th century, reached prominence in arts and letters in the 13th century, turning into the epicenter for the Persian scholars and artists, notable among them, Hafez and Saadi. During the Zand dynasty in the 18th century, when Persia stretched from Afghanistan to Armenia, Shiraz was chosen as the capital of the empire. This magical city has always been known as the city of literature, poetry, gardens, and wine. At one time, it had also been a prized sanctuary for Jews and Christians.

Shiraz is particularly famous for being near Pasargadae (90 kilometers to the northeast of Shiraz), the seat of the Achaemenid Empire (550 B.C.), founded by Cyrus the Great, the much-cherished iconic king of Persia.

Cyrus is mentioned 23 times by name in the Bible as the deliverer of the Jews from the Babylonian captivity. Upon freeing the Jews, he is known to have decreed that the Temple in Jerusalem may be rebuilt and that the previously captive Jews can return to their land for that purpose. Moreover, he had helped them rebuild the Temple by sending back the sacred vessels which had been taken from the First Temple along with a considerable sum of money to pay for its construction. This had marked a great epoch in the history of the Jewish people. According to Isaiah 45:1 of the Hebrew Bible, God anointed Cyrus for this task, even referring to him as a messiah, the anointed one, the only non-Jewish figure in the

Bible to be called so.

Cyrus had created the largest empire the world had yet seen, extending from the Mediterranean Sea in the west to the Indus River in the east. The administration of the empire through satraps under the central government in Pasargadae had been exemplary at the time. Furthermore, his respect for the customs and religions practiced in the lands he had conquered had endeared him to his subjects, strengthening his rule.

He is recognized for his achievements in human rights, politics, and military strategy, influencing both Eastern and Western civilizations. It has been written that the Persian influence in the ancient world had extended as far as Athens, where upper-class Athenians are known to have adopted certain aspects of the culture of Persia's ruling class. As for human rights, the proclamation inscribed onto the ancient artifact known as the Cyrus Cylinder is popularized as the oldest known declaration of human rights.

To this day, Cyrus continues to play a crucial role in defining the national identity of modern Iran. He is an enormously popular figure amongst modern Iranians. His tomb serves as a spot of reverence for millions of Iranian youths, craving for their lost national identity—and much to the chagrin of today's Islamic regime in Iran too.

In Shiraz, we lived in my paternal grandfather's house located in the well-known district of Blackstone Bazaar, an established and reputable part of Shiraz. I have memories going back to when I was only four years old.

In those days, most houses had large and heavy wooden portals, which were adorned with two heavy iron knockers called *kolouns*, used for knocking. Approaching our house through the *kouche*, the narrow walkway outside, a giant portal, flanked by two niches, one on each side, stuck out.

The front door opened to a *hashti*, a small vestibule that separated the main frontal entrance from the courtyard inside. Past the hashti, a large cobblestoned courtyard, featuring a large and deep, inscrutable pool in the middle, was reached. On each side of the pool, a verdant garden was cultivated, hosting old tangerine and sour-orange trees that majestically reached the second-floor windows.

There was a two-story brick building on each side of the courtyard. They were connected by a long, underground basement beneath the courtyard. During summers, the basement was used as a cooled, living area, where refuge was taken from the excruciating heat outside, and in the wintertime, it was used as a cooled pantry and a quasi-refrigerator, where provisions and preserves made the summer before were kept from spoiling.

In such a large household, traditional custom called for two domestics. We had Bemoon Jan, an old maid, who had served our family since before my father was born, and Golestan, a young, strong freed black female slave, who managed most of the laborious housework, including cleaning, cooking, and gardening.

The kitchen and the restroom were on one side, opposite the front entrance, between the two residential buildings, and set some distance apart from each other. An old wood-burning stove was used for cooking in the kitchen. The restroom was a dark and spooky joint that we children could only dare frequent with a maid, lantern in hand, guiding. My paternal aunt, her husband, and their three children lived in the building on the left side. My paternal grandparents occupied the ground floor of the building on the right side, above which our family of five lived.

I remember, my aunt's husband had a hand wind-up gramophone, which blurted out old, nostalgic songs that we children longed to listen to. On my father's side, I had two more aunts and two more uncles, who lived in their own separate houses.

My parents were cousins. When they married, Father was twenty and Mother was three years older, which was an oddity then because most grooms were typically much older than their brides. Unlike most marriages that were arranged by others, I would someday learn that their marriage had grown out of love. Father was madly in love with Mother. Mother was a teacher, which was also a rarity at the time when women were not much more than confined to their houses, and most were not even allowed a rudimentary education.

"How was she a teacher in those retrograde times?" you might ask.

I would have to say, "She was endowed with a sway for education and courageously dared to delve into that realm in the face of endemic opposition."

She was exceptionally refined, talented, and tasteful, and as a socialite, the talk and pride of the extended family.

She was also gifted with poetic proclivities. I was too young to discern that her poetry would one day be a treasure trove for her progeny, or I would have collected them. She composed poetry for each of us children, perceptively relating it to a different flower. The only ode composed by her that has stayed with me through the years is the quatrain that she, overtaken by the innocent look on my face while lulling me to sleep, came up with, impromptu,

> *One night, I held an angel snoozing in my arms*
> *Where in heaven such fair angel? I wondered.*
> *Lullaby, the look on her face was...*
> *Lucky he, who slept with such angel till dawn*

As a child, before falling asleep in the intoxicating, balmy air outside, I would, along with my siblings, pray and recite a famous verse (Ayatolkorsi – Surah Al-Baqarah: 255) from the Holy Quran that my mother had taught us. Vocalizing my litany while looking onto that clear, deep-blue summer sky unique to Shiraz, full of countless twinkling shiny stars, I would become mesmerized with the grandiose scene before my eyes. I would try to locate and count the major stars: Polaris, Sirius, Rigel, Vega. I could not help but fall into deep thought, desperately trying to fathom where the sky started and where it ended. One thing would lead to another, arousing my consciousness further and further. I would often wonder about the depth of the inscrutable universe beyond the milky galaxy and my little place in the grand scheme of things. This, I believe, was the beginning of my inclination towards divinity. A dim inkling to the answer would begin to take shape during my formative years, only to be crystalizing when I would be taken in by the letter and spirit of the Holy Scriptures many years hence.

I had a brother named Farzad who was three years older than me, and when I was three years old, my sister, Parvaneh, was born.

Kidnapping

*"But that I am forbid to tell the secrets of my prison-
house, I could a tale unfold whose lightest word
would harrow up thy soul, freeze thy young blood...,"*

~ Shakespeare

Television and radio did not exist in those days. Toys were a rarity too. The only toy I owned was made by Bemoon Jan, our old maid. It was a Barbie-like doll made of cloth that had a coin as its face. I joyously played with it for hours on end. I sometimes sat on one of the two niches to either side of the front door with searching eyes upon pedestrians and often gazed off down the alley, daydreaming, passing time, and waiting for Mother to return home from school.

One day, as I sat on one of those infamous niches, observing people walking by, lost in thought, a veiled woman with deep-set eyes under henna-dyed eyebrows approached me.

"Your mother has sent me to take you to see her at school," she warmly whispered into my ear.

I beamed with excitement and, without thinking of telling anyone in the house, took the woman's extended hand and, with jaunty steps, walked away with her. She tightly clasped my hand in hers and walked me through countless crooked and weaving alleys until we reached a wide gravel road. I would later learn that the name of that eerie thoroughfare was "Manouchehri".

She motioned a rattling horse drawn-carriage to stop. I was too young to know that my mother did not ride to the school she taught at. We stepped in, the coachman slapped his reins, and the carriage started off with a sudden jolt on a long bumpy ride. We rode for a long time that felt like an eternity. The carriage finally stopped. We stepped out, and she paid the coachman.

She waited until the carriage, leaving a cloud of dust behind, was well out of sight. Then she suddenly pounced on me and, with one swift jerking move, pulled the golden earrings (that were knitted to my ears, so that I would not lose them) from my ears. Blood gushed out of my torn ears. I felt a sharp pain piercing through me and started to sob as my shoulders felt the warmth of the blood. She nonchalantly cast her evil eyes on me.

"Hush, I'm going to bring your mother, stay put, don't move," she blurted threateningly and quickly walked off.

Trembling, I followed her with soaked eyes until she shrank to a tiny dark speck against the hazy sky and disappeared into the grey dusty distance...and vanished into thin air.

After sobbing for a long time, I fell silent of exhaustion. I was weak of hunger, thirst, and fear, and my weary limbs finally giving way, I collapsed onto the ground.

My family, relatives, and friends, who had by now learned of my disappearance, had begun frantically to search for me. Word had arrived home that a three-year-old girl had been sighted in a desolate place; this rumor must have been spread by that same woman, who probably knew my family.

Finally, a family member found me and carried my numb and cold body home on his shoulders. Due to the lack of telephones in those days, others, not having been informed I was found, kept on searching for me until, exhausted and downcast, they returned home and saw me. Overcome by joy, they enthusiastically kept on hugging and kissing me. Mother was on her knees, prostrating in supplication, kissing the ground, and profusely thanking God.

"Dear Lord, thank you, thank you...thank you that only her earrings were taken, and thank you for giving her back to us, or else we don't know what we would have done," she kept on saying while tears of joy were streaming down her cheeks.

I never, again, sat on that wicked niche outside. I remained home content playing with the only toy I owned in my entire world, my little doll.

In the absence of toys to play with, we were happy and satisfied with the simplest plays, such as hide and seek, or tag. Even having been held up high by an elder, so we could pick a tangerine from the prolific citrus trees in the garden, was regarded as a grand play!

In the summers, despite unbearable heat, we were scared to take a dip in the pool, for it was deep, murky, and creepy.

In the afternoons, after the midday breeze generously cooled the air, under the lush branches of the tangerine and the sour-orange trees, a few wide wooden beds were usually covered with rugs by our maid, Golestan, on which elaborate afternoon tea was spread. It invariably featured a samovar, unceasingly brewing black tea, alongside a spread containing unleavened flatbread, hot from the local bakery, feta cheese, seasonal fruits, thin crunchy cucumbers, ripe tomatoes, crisp leafy lettuce, and vinegar syrup, used to dip the lettuce in.

Kids ate and played boisterously. Grandparents ate and dozed off. Others ate, talked, and told heartfelt stories. At nightfall, as the bright moon rose high among a zillion twinkling stars against the dark sky, my grandparents spread their beds and conveniently slept there, enjoying the fresh cool air permeated with the heavenly smells of citrus and flowers.

Maternal Grandmother

"I was a child and she was a child, in this kingdom by the sea, but we loved with a love that was more than love, I & my Annabel Lee...,"

~ E. A. Poe

We always looked forward to and enjoyed visiting our maternal grandmother, who was a widow. She lived in a quaint old house that belonged to her brother who, after her husband was killed, had taken upon himself the task of supporting her and her two young children, my mother and my uncle. The entrance to the house was similar to ours, a large and heavy portal, which opened to a hashti adjoining a cobblestoned courtyard. But the courtyard was more expansive with buildings erected on three sides.

My grandmother lived with her son (my uncle) and his family of three children in one building. Her brother (my mother's uncle) lived with his family of four children in another building.

In the afternoons when the sun lazily went down and the cooler air rushed in, the wooden beds in the courtyard were covered with rugs, and the luxuriant flowers were watered, which further cooled the air and pervaded it with the intoxicating scent of flowers.

As the afternoon wore on well into the night, we languorously lounged on those beds, feasting on afternoon tea and the customary myriad of munchies that accompanied it. It felt as if time had come to a crawl and did not matter anymore.

There was a large, shallow pool in the middle of the courtyard, painted in bright turquoise color. How delightful was that pool? I have etched on my mind many fond memories of playing in that innocuous pool, chasing small redfish, frantically swimming away from us in all directions. How enjoyable were dabbling, running, and chasing in those sparkly and blissful waters?

To one end of the courtyard stood an old persimmon tree with heavy branches humbly bent down, loaded with ripe juicy persimmons, availing themselves to our small eager hands.

I also recall that not everything in that house was benign. In the far corner of the basement, near the kitchen above, there was a deep coverless well that incited great awe in us. It could have easily claimed a life by a mere mishap. Once the underground rain-water filled the well, the excess water flowed through a dug channel and filled the pool outside. We often played hide and seek near that unfathomable well, unknowingly inviting a tragedy. In hindsight, it gives me chills to think about what might have happened if one of us fell in that pit of a well.

My maternal grandfather had been a prominent feudal landowner. He had owned much arable, agricultural land, which was plowed, tilled, and maintained by his vassals, producing a variety of crops. His love for land and agriculture had been insatiable. Whenever any of his brothers needed to sell any land, he would unhesitatingly volunteer to buy some. His brothers had asked him one day,

"You own so much land, way more than all of us combined. Why do you want more?"

He had returned with a derisive grin,

"I want to have enough land to last through my next seven generations of progeny!"

Little did he know that the reeling world spins us as it deems, and he was no exception. He was to be no more than an itinerant actor in this grand theatrical called life, with only a short, appointed role to play.

***

> *"Say, only what God has decreed will happen to us...He is our Master...let the believers put their trust in God...,"*
>
> ~ *H. Quran*

One day, while inspecting his vast properties, his life came to an abrupt and tragic end when a bullet pierced through his heart. No one knew who had shot him. Some said it was a hunter's bullet that had accidentally hit him. Others claimed it was one of his disgruntled vassals, who had taken revenge upon him.

When tragedy struck, grandmother had been young and beautiful. Mother and uncle were only four and five years old. As I have mentioned, soon after Grandfather died, they were graciously taken in by Grandmother's brother as their caretaker. Despite Grandfather's grandiose wishes for his family, their lives were to be rendered asunder with the painful loss of a caring husband and father. Alas, deprived of a loving husband who had been her pillar of support throughout her short-married life, her golden years, Grandmother remained mournful from her budding days to the waning days of her life. She later died of old age, nevertheless.

***

> *"...all manifestation from the One is return to the One...all separation is union...all otherness is sameness...all plenitude is the void...,"*
>
> ~ *S. H. Nasr*

Move to Fasa

*"A dark unfathomed tide...of interminable pride...a
mystery & a dream, should my early life seem...,"*

~ E. A. Poe

The ever-reeling world spun us at will from one place to another. When I was five years old, Father, who worked for the Ministry of Finance, was transferred to Fasa, a small town about 125 kilometers southeast of Shiraz.

After we moved to Fasa, Mother started to teach at the local school for girls. We first lived in a snug little house, which conveniently bordered the school where mother taught. We then moved to a larger, a la mode house that had two buildings across from each other; one on each side of the courtyard; and luxuriant gardens in between. In the middle of the courtyard, a large and deep pool was dug.

Father often took me on his leisurely walks in the pristine countryside, in the green rolling open plains, under the wide expanse of clear blue sky. The air was inebriating.

***

*"When I strike the open plains, something happens.
I'm home. I breathe differently, that love of great
spaces, of rolling open country like the sea...it's the
great passion of my life...,"*

~ Willa Cather

The pastoral scenes we walked into were a delight to the eye. Overcome with poetic effusions in that ideal setting, on each excursion, Father would recite two odes to me to leave to memory; asking me to recite them back to him on the following trip; and two more odes, he would recite, once I memorized the first two. The following quatrain readily comes to my mind,

No dates, gotten...from the bush, planted
No silk, woven...from the wool, spun
No repentances...recorded
No noble deeds...recorded

***

"Poetry is an act of generosity...,"

~ Don Skiles

Night Stories in Fasa

"North & West are crumbling...thrones falling,
kingdoms trembling...come, flee away to purer East,
there on patriarch's air to feast...to the depths
whence all things rise...,"

~ *Goethe*

Nights were not short of magical in Fasa. The stories I heard there as a child form some of the happiest memories of my childhood that have stayed with me all these years.

We had a maid named Khatoon Jan and a servant named Ali Mohammad who, although illiterate, was a glib talker with an impeccable command of speech, that "supremely human gift." He was a natural storyteller with an elephant memory; a raconteur par excellence you might say. He could have been a William Faulkner!

On clear starry nights, as the stars twinkled, he would give fodder to my young imagination by recounting ancient Iranian legendary stories, such as "The King of Angels", "The Dark Chained Monster", "Rostam e Dastan",- and "Zahak and his Pet Snakes", who were daily fed brains of two slain young boys.

***

"Night, the reserved, the reticent, gives more than it
takes...,"

~ *John Ashbery*

With sparkle flashing in his eyes, his pupils dilating, and his animated mouth moving unceasingly, he told us stories with such minute detail and lucid description that immersed us in awe, wonder, and joy.

The stories he told were skillfully elongated with such constant turn of events that he never ran out of material. In lieu of television or radio, we waited for his stories every night with great anticipation.

His stories were invariably climactic in genre. As his imaginary cast of characters took their endless adventurous twist and turns, and we listening moonstruck, the tension would come to a high pitch. Then a cut would come, keeping the climax of the story for the following night, leaving us fascinated, mesmerized, and in unbearable waiting. They remind me of today's soap operas or Walt Disney movies!

His cast of characters always ventured into dangerous odysseys. They would be entangled, needing help. Then a genie would always appear to overcome the antagonist and save the protagonist. Dark Chained Monster would be blown to pieces by the genie. We were left spellbound, with imagination at full play!

***

"Ever let the fancy roam! Pleasure never is at home...,"

~ *John Keats*

Summer Fun

"Bribed with a little sunlight & a few prismatic tints, we bless our Maker & stave off his wrath with hymns...,"

~ Henry D. Thoreau

"Ah, summer, what power you have to make us suffer & like it...,"

~ Russell Baker

Summers were the happy occasions when with every excuse, families gathered in droves to perform various functions with much mirth.

There were days when a donkey-load of sour grapes called, *ghoureh*, was unloaded. We, young and old, would gather in large numbers to extract the green acerbic juice. First, we would pick the sour grapes, separating them from the stems by hand, which was a lengthy process, affording the grown-ups plenty of time to catch up on chitchat and to "propitiating the tongue of gossip," and could use as many hands as were available. Then the washing of a heap of sour grapes would ensue. After washing, they would be pressed by a hired man, using his pressing machine, and poured into many long and wide bottles, called *gharabeh*, to keep for the yearly need.

Then time to make tomato paste would come. After washing the red ripe tomatoes, fresh from the farm, they would be mashed in large, round copper trays by hand and kept for a day to allow time for the tomatoes to sink to the bottom and for the water to rise to the top. After that, they would go through strainers, poured into huge copper pots, and boiled slowly into a paste on a wood-burning stove.

The paste would be ladled out into large and round flat copper trays, called *majmaa*, and kept in the sun for a few days to further thicken. The thick tomato paste was finally transferred into large carafes and kept in the cooled basement pantry, for use throughout the year.

Summer's end was time for the lemons. Crates of lemon would arrive on donkeys. They were first washed. A hired man would arrive with his juicer machine. The lemons were sliced in halves and pressed. Then many gharabehs were filled with lemon juice, to be used in the year to come.

Cooking oil was processed in early spring. One *kharvar*, equivalent to 300 kilograms, of freshly churned butter would arrive. Butter was boiled in large pots and turned into liquid cooking oil and poured into rectangular aluminum containers known as *halabs*, which were then sealed, only to be opened when the time came to use. The residue left in the cooking pot was tartly and delicious, which we children scraped with hand and licked with gusto.

I vividly remember our house in Fasa. My parents' bedroom was at one end of the building to the right side of the courtyard. Next to it, we had our formal living room, where guests were hosted and entertained. It led to a small adjoining anteroom called a *ghooshvareh*, which connected that building to an adjacent one. In the adjacent building, this same anteroom opened to a casual living room that was turned into a makeshift bedroom at night for us children. A narrow and dark walkway connected this room to a repository, which was used to keep such preserves and provisions as lemon extract, vinegar, and melons.

We also had a long, cooled basement down below that was highly sought after during sizzling summer months.

I, wholeheartedly, miss that congenial atmosphere, that idyllic lifestyle that was uniquely simple, real, tangible, and palpable; that pulsated with a voluptuous vibe; a house teeming with family and friends and their endemic folkways and their supremely "all-too-human" interactions, socializing, eating, talking, and telling stories.

Oftentimes, we children enjoyed chasing a warped plastic ball all day in the courtyard with zeal. Farzad invariably emerged as the winner and never hesitated to brag about it either.

"One day, my kid will tell your kid that: my father always beat your mother, so I've to beat you too," he would say with a mocking smile.

Ironically, since my daughter, Setareh, would happen to be older than his son, Fardad, and they would never get to be playmates, his wish was never granted!

With the balmy weather, picnicking was the order of the day during those slumberous holidays and on weekends. Ali Mohammad, our servant, used to fasten a rope between two trees, low enough, so we could sit on and swing. Then with one push from behind, we would lose balance, somersault in the air, and hit the ground. This play was called *abrang*, in the local vernacular.

When picnicking in the countryside, one other fun and mischievous thing we reveled in was making forays upon fruit trees, which were guarded behind orchard walls. I remember the fruit laden branches, voluptuously protruding over dilapidated mud walls, teasing us, revealing their readiness to be picked: cherries, apples, peaches... For some unfathomable reason, those forbidden fruits were far more pleasing to our palates than the ones Ali Mohammad paid for at the market!

Drowning Incident

"Nor does the man sitting by the hearth beneath his roof better escape his fated doom...,"

~ Aeschylus.

Springs and summers were generally imbued with lots of fun. They were times for playing, basking in the sun, and passing lazy afternoons lounging on beds in the courtyard well into the night; eating, talking, hearing stories, inhaling the delicious flower-scented air, and sleeping in the fresh cool air under the starry sky outside.

Summers were times when families enjoyed events akin to food festivals. They were occasions for preparing provisions and preserves for the winter. We were full of life and vigor, and we were happy. But there were unpleasant moments too that shook us at times.

I will never forget the infamous pool with its inscrutable depths that silently sat in the middle of the courtyard...

I remember one day when my mother was nursing my younger sister Fataneh in the cooled basement below, something horrible happened. Fataneh and Fatah were both born in Fasa. But tragically, we would lose Fatah to jaundice at the age of seven.

The sun was scorching hot. Farzad could not resist taking a dip in the pool. The pool was deep and covered the grown-ups to shoulder height. I looked at him enjoying the cold water. I somehow mustered the courage to sit on the shallow step inside the pool, dangling my legs in the water. As I was enjoying myself, wading in the water, humming, my gaze fell upon my younger sister, Parvaneh, who seemed to be envying me.

"Parvaneh, you wanna come too?" said I.

It was as if she had impatiently been waiting to join me.

"Yes, yes. I do, I do. I'm coming," she returned eagerly. She ran toward me delightedly.

"Can I sit next to you?" she asked peevishly.

"Yeah."

She sat next to me in the pool.

The step we sat on was slippery with moss. As we joyfully kicked the water with our legs, she suddenly slipped and plunged headlong into the water. I reached out to grab her, but lost my balance and fell into the water too. Neither of us could swim. Water covered us. We desperately gasped for air. Farzad was already out of the pool, drying himself to put on his clothes. He had noticed the lurid scene as he was turning to go inside. He hastily jumped in the pool to save us.

"Oh no, oh no..." he kept on yelling.

But he had been overcome by paralyzing fear and shock, rendering him unable to swim, and he started to drown himself.

Mother, who had heard Farzad screaming, had hurried up the stairs from the basement, facing her three children drowning,

"Oh no. Oh, God. Oh, God. Oh no..."

She jumped into the pool with her clothes on and was able to reach me first. With a tenacious grip, she grabbed me by the arm and put me on the ledge of the pool. She saved Farzad next. But little Parvaneh had disappeared into the murky waters and could not be seen. Mother kept searching and searching, shrieking and shrieking.

"Parvaneh... Parvaneh..."

Finally, her hand felt Parvaneh's numb body, floating deep in the water. She grabbed her, put her numb body outside the pool, and barely managed to drag herself out. Poor Mother, due to the hysteria and exertion, collapsed onto the ground, unconscious and near-lifeless. And Parvaneh did not move either. Her stomach had badly swollen. Farzad and I quickly picked her up by her feet. Water started pouring out of her mouth, then she began to gasp for air. But we were losing our mother. Farzad kept screaming.

"Mother, please, Mother, please wake up... we're all alive, see... see... Parvaneh is alive too...here she is...please," he kept on pleading with a coarse voice and tearful eyes.

After some dreadful moments that seemed like a lifetime, Mother finally opened her eyes, reached out to us, hugged the three of us in her arms, and pressed us tightly against her pounding heart. We all huddled and sobbed uncontrollably for a long time...

It was an unforgettable and terrifying day. Coincidently, that day, our domestics were not home either. Looking back, I am still baffled by my dear mother's heroic action, who like a lioness saved the three of us. I can only attribute it to a miracle of divine grace, a clear dispensation of divine providence.

***

"Every moment of light & dark is a miracle...,"

~ Walt Whitman

My thoughts snap back to my childhood. Mother always took me with her to the school, where she taught. I was too young to attend school myself. I meandered in the schoolyard and, with perceptive eyes, observed students who reluctantly sauntered to classrooms when the bell rang and rushed out wildly with raucous shrieks of joy when the bell rang again, swarming in the courtyard during breaks, chattering raucously, buzzing like bees.

Teachers took a liking to me. I joined them when they gathered in the office during breaks, talking, and sipping tea from tiny *estekan* glasses over lumpy sugar cubs, or sometimes pouring the tea in the saucers and drinking thereof.

As we approached *Nowruz*, the Iranian New Year, the office was ornately decorated with colorful, silky drapery, which one day caught my eye. I fancied that beautiful drapery so much that one day, out of the blue, I asked the woman principal if I could have a piece of it.

"This is so pretty. I really like this. Can I have this piece?" I bashfully pleaded.

"Sure, you can, sweetie," returned the principal, vacantly.

She then left the room. Not knowing better, I thought she meant what she said. I then meticulously folded the piece I liked and tucked it away in my backpack. After I got home, I hid it in a safe place without telling anyone.

A year passed and time to decorate the office for Nowruz came again. After searching for the missing drapery piece to no avail, the principal asked each teacher reproachfully of its whereabouts. The teachers took offense, naturally. I overheard my parents one night broaching the subject.

"An expensive piece of decorative cloth has been missing at school. No one knows anything about it and we're all distressed," Mother confided with Father.

"I have it," I interjected quickly.

"What? You have it? How? What're you talking about?" Mother asked quizzically.

"Yeah, I have it. I liked it a lot when I first saw it in the office last year. And when they were putting them away, I asked the lady principal if I could have a piece and she said yes, so I took it," I mumbled innocently.

"Well, Dearie, she must have just said it, not meaning to. She isn't allowed to give away school property. Go and bring me the piece, please," Mother said with a sigh of relief.

I fetched the piece sourly. Mother returned it to the school the next day, gave it to the lady principal, and recounted all that had transpired. Everyone had at once been relieved and amused by her story. An epic misunderstanding was explained away! I, early on, learned the meaning of baseless, perfunctory courtesies. I learned that one should not say anything that one does not mean. It is a pity that people still say things they do not mean.

But this ritual of courtesy known as *taarof* is deeply embedded in the Iranian culture. Taarof is known to have originally emanated from the Iranian concept of hospitality, requiring a host to offer anything a guest might want while a guest is equally obliged to refuse it. This back-and-forth process of offer and refusal usually repeats itself several times (usually three times) before the host and the guest finally determine whether the host's offer and the guest's refusal are genuine, or simply a show of politeness.

Those who have come in contact with Iranians often say that taarof is one of the most fundamental things to understand about the Iranian culture. Not a few times have non-Iranian tourists visiting Iran been confused and misinterpreted taarof. For instance, there have been instances when paying for cab fares that they have misconstrued cab drivers' taarofs (offers of non-payment), saying, "No. It is not worthy of you," for granted and walked off without paying – only to be surprised shortly after, when realizing that the offer had not been in earnest!

Brother, Farzad, and his Antics

*"Tree you are, moss you are, you are violets with
wind above them...a child...so high... you are & all
this is folly to the world...,"*

~ *Ezra Pound*

My brother, Farzad, always reveled in pulling insidious pranks on us, poking fun, and having a good time. He never ran out of shenanigans either. He had a nickname for each of us, which he scathingly called us by, just to agitate us, starting a commotion that embroiled everyone in a family strife with Parvaneh and I ending up crying and complaining to Mother, who always had to mitigate to calm us down. He had a knack for, in a tone too serious not to believe, telling us imaginary, baseless stories. One time he called us to reveal a special secret.

"I gotta come clean and tell you all something that you aren't supposed to know on account of being kids and all," he jested one day, staring at us with dilated eyes.

"Really? Please tell me *dadash* (brother) Farzad. I promise I won't tell anyone," I returned pleadingly.

"What about her?"

"Who? Parvaneh?"

"Yeah."

"I promise I won't tell either," Parvaneh pledged.

"OK. Listen and listen carefully, because I'm gonna tell you all once and it's something that no one else is supposed to know, understand?" Farzad said, sharp-eyed.

"Yes, we do," we promised.

"We have an older brother, whom you don't know anything about. His name is…. He's living in Europe, studying….," he concocted with a scornful grin.

We listened with awe. It was too shocking a revelation not to be shaken by, and we had to get to the bottom of it. After days of suspense, petrified, we asked Mother if we had a second brother. She denied it all.

"Mother, I think they're old enough to know. Tell them the truth," Farzad persisted unabashedly. As always, a simmering family maelstrom was to loom, and much yelling and crying was to follow.

Now, in hindsight, I think Farzad must have been entertaining thoughts of his own future plans, setting his sights on attending school in Europe, because after graduating from high school, he wasted no time in pursuing higher education in Germany and graduated with an engineering degree in mining.

And after completing university, accompanied by his beautiful German girlfriend, Oteh, he returned home from Germany. Oteh was tall, blond, and had captivating hazelnut eyes. Their return ushered in yet a happy period in our lives. Not knowing her tongue, communication turned out to be a challenging task. Surprisingly, of all the people, mother best managed to communicate with her.

"Oteh likes walnuts," Mother announced one day.

"How do you know mother?"

"She told me herself. I asked Oteh what she likes and she said 'walnuts'!"

We tried our best to make sure she had a good time while she stayed with us in Iran. We took her to visit the Iranian historical sites, but she was not much impressed. She decided not to stay with us after all. Oddly enough, she proved to be a zealously patriotic and proud German, who preferred her homeland to ours.

"There's a special providence in the fall of a sparrow...," Hamlet

Once she left, Mother and I began to find Farzad a wife among relatives and friends we knew. At the time, it was incumbent upon mothers and sisters to search for brides for their sons and brothers. After much searching, we found a suitable mate in a nice girl by the name of Fariba.

She happened to be the daughter of an army general who had recently moved to Shiraz on a military assignment. It was one of those things that I believe was predestined. We were relieved and delighted that we had finally found a wonderful wife for Farzad.

After they were married in a lavish ceremony, duty happened to call for Farzad to temporarily go out of town, so he asked me to watch over his new bride while he was away. And because of my deep-seated affection for my brother, I did my best to take care of her, keeping her company in his absence. We spent much quality time together, shopping, and talking. I told her all I could about my brother's traits and habits, because after all, this had been an arranged marriage, and she did not know my brother all that well.

A year later they had a son, Fardad, and two years hence, a daughter, Azar. My brother established a successful mining engineering company that was awarded lucrative contracts by the government for work on various modernization projects. He had a sizable staff in his employment. He also had a full-time chauffeur. And therefore, his wife Fariba, never learned to drive, and when Farzad's business came to a temporary halt during the 1979 revolution, with the driver gone and not ever having had to learn how to drive, she was at a loss!

Nonetheless, he stayed in Iran to serve his country. He successfully drilled numerous artesian aquifer wells that did not need any pumps in bringing the underground water to the surface. These wells were especially needed for the irrigation of crops in the arid terrains of central Iran. Even today, at his old age, despite a debilitating eye illness known as macular degeneration, he has not retired yet and continues to live an active life.

Theatre in Fasa

"...the world's a stage & all man &
women...players...they have their exits & entrances &
one man in his time plays many parts...,"

~ Hamlet

Our simple, unadulterated world lacked entertainment in the form of television or motion pictures. But live performance was rampant. Itinerant theatrical repertoires often came to our little town, enlivening our lives. Father, who was a high-ranking government official in the Ministry of Finance, was given the best seats when those plays came to town. At a young age, I had difficulty understanding the plays. But I enjoyed the intermezzos, and afterward, practiced them passionately at home. I remember one that went like this,

For a single bean...How long should I keep on coming
& going...? Coming & going...? And yet this is full of
sand & in war with my teeth...Full of sand & in war
with my teeth...

With the advent of cinema, a whole new chapter in my young imaginative mind began. I was immersed with the acting on the screen, deeply impinging upon my untamed imagination.

But before then, summer afternoons were often spent in the lazy open air, eating, chatting, and playing. As the days wore on, the sun dropping in the horizon and the moon beginning to ascend against the clear blue sky, we lounged on the wooden beds in the courtyard, under the trees. With night falling, we usually spread our sleeping beds outside, and slept tightly in the pleasant summer air.

I remember we kept a young and playful lamb in the courtyard one summer. While I was fast asleep one night, I happened to slowly slide to the edge of the bed, and then rolled out of the bed. I fell and hit the ground hard with a loud bang that gave that poor lamb quite a jolt, and started it off running amok around the courtyard in circles with no respite. The loud sound of jingles around its neck filled the air and woke everyone up. Everyone fretfully jumped out of bed. Father, half-naked, hair sticking out, had to chase that poor lamb down. To rein it in, he had to keep running after it for a long time. And the frightened lamb was madly sprinting in circles! It was a comical scene, which is still vivid in my memory, and it cracks me up laughing every time I remember that hilarious episode!

***

"...all that we see or seem is but a dream within a dream...,"

~ *E.A. Poe*

Nowruz Preparations

*"Oh land, I'll build you again, if, with bricks of my life.
I'll build pillars for your roof, if, with my own bones.
I'll inhale the perfume of flower, favored by your
youth, again. I'll wash the blood off of you with my
tears, again...,"*

~ Simin Behbehani

*"O Earth. O Earth. Return! Arise from the dewy
grass...,"*

~ William Blake

Nowruz, which means "new day", is the Iranian New Year. It has been celebrated for over 7,000 years. It is the day of the March (or vernal) equinox and marks the beginning of the spring in the Northern Hemisphere. This moment that the Sun crosses the celestial equator and equalizes night and day is celebrated by Iranians who observe it with their traditional rituals.

According to the ancient Iranian scientist Tusi, the first day of the Iranian New Year is the day on which the sun enters Aries before noon.

Nowruz is also deeply embedded in Iranian religions, such as Mithraism and Zoroastrianism. In Mithraism especially, festivals had a deep linkage with the Sun's light.

Xenophon has written of the Nowruz celebrations taking place in Persepolis, an important day according to him, during the rule of Achaemenid Empire (550–330 B.C.). On that day, kings of the Achaemenid nations brought gifts to the King of Kings. The palace of Apadana in the Persepolis complex had been built for the specific purpose of celebrating Nowruz, hosting other subject kings who had arrived to pay their respects to the King of Kings on this special occasion.

A few months before Nowruz, Mother always began to prepare for the holiday festivities, which among other things included baking the traditional Iranian sweet delicacies. Baking supplies were not readily available in those days. Baking essentials, such as sugar powder, blanched almonds, diced pistachios, and chickpea flour known as *nokhodchi*, were not sold in the market. They had to be made at home from scratch. Baking was still considered a closely guarded family art, requiring creativity, ingenuity, and experience.

Mother's epicurean baking was the talk of the family and the friends. We children were recruited by her when baking confectioneries for Nowruz got underway. Farzad was usually tasked with blanching the almonds and tending the fire in the stove, constantly adjusting it to suit the required heat for baking different items. Parvaneh was in charge of cleaning the mess, washing and putting away dishes and utensils. And I, standing close to Mother's side, served as an assistant to her while she was orchestrating the whole show.

Once the Nowruz sweets were baked and cooled off for a day, they were placed in large cardboard boxes and stored away in the repository next to our casual living room, not to be touched again till the new year arrived. The repository was locked and, entrusted with its custodianship, I was tendered the key, to which I tightly held till the appointed day, as if I was not a child! Despite my diligence, the sweets were not totally immune to Farzad or Parvaneh's occasional forays.

Other traditional functions related to the new year included making the sweet bread and the *samanu*.

The baking of the sweet bread took a few days. A lady baker would come to make the dough on a certain day. For her to show up, Mother had to call her days in advance, begging her to fit us in her busy Nowruz schedule. She was one heavyset, bad-tempered lady.

After the dough was made, it sat for a day to rise. The next day, she would return for the actual baking. The baking paraphernalia, such as large pans and wood boards, were set in place. The wood-burning stove was calibrated to emit the proper heat. Then the actual baking would commence. The lady baker had to have a few assistants at her elbow to pick up, with care and one by one, the bread from the cooking pans and place them in a designated place. I was always a ready volunteer as an assistant, but would soon get tired.

We children were in awe of that commanding baker and did not dare to misbehave in her presence. She promised us that when the baking was completed, if we were not intemperate, she would make us each a special bread. This was an added incentive for us to stay obedient throughout the baking process.

After baking the bread was completed, it would be time to make a special holiday sweet called samanu, or as we said in Shiraz, samani.

The making of samanu was an arduous task. First, wheat had to be soaked in water well in advance to grow sprouts. After sprouts were grown and roots were formed, they were grinded by pounding in a large a stone bowl called a *havang*. Then the ground wheat was squeezed in a fine net to extract out the sap. The wheat's sap was poured into a huge pot and heated on fire. All the while, the mixture was stirred by a long wooden ladle skin to a snow shovel. The heating and the stirring continued for almost 24 hours, by which time the color of the mixture would have turned brown. During that time, almonds and walnuts were consistently added to the mix.

The nights on which samanu was made, relatives, friends, and neighbors flocked to our house with lit candles to take their turns in stirring the samanu, all the while praying for their wishes to come true, which in a way sacralized the event.

This time-consuming process was far from easy. It was also an all-inclusive, collective affair. It had family, friends, and neighbors participating. The event would evolve into a festival, a social event, starting with dinner that mother had prepared for the multitude of guests who arrived at night to stir the samanu and invoke the heavens for their heartfelt wishes to be granted. Stirring would last till daybreak. At dawn, the samanu was apportioned and poured into the bowls that the attendees had brought. They were then distributed among family and friends.

The making of the samanu was, in a way, quite symbolic. It was emblematic of a higher principle. It was also a social event. It denoted the coming together for a common human purpose. Despite the rudimentary lifestyle of that day and age, the making of the samanu was an event that evoked togetherness, spirituality, and ultimately love. A simple event as that was, as all other traditional events were, a cause for closer human relations.

Unfortunately, in today's digital age, human contact suffices to sending a mere picture or a short caption via a mobile or a computer to loved ones while we are all wide apart. Less and less time is nowadays spent with family and friends. Seeing one another in person and face to face has become a rarity. I believe that perhaps the only social benefit of today's digital age is to keep us momentarily abreast of the world events as they unfold.

On the morning of the new year, the baked goods were artfully arranged in colorful dishes of different sizes and shapes and set on the living room tables, to be savored by the throng of guests, who would start swarming right after the new year was announced. About an hour or so before the new year, we would all change into our newest clothes, bought or made only once a year just for Nowruz. Everyone, already bathed and groomed and in new clothes, would gather around the Nowruz spread, called *haft-sin*, which had been beautifully displayed on a *Termeh* cloth days in advance. We would await with excitement the exact moment of the March equinox to celebrate the new year.

The haft-sin spread was comprised of seven (haft) items beginning with the letter sin, "s":

Sabze: wheat, barley, or lentil sprouts, grown in a dish

Samanu: sweet pudding made from wheat germ

Senjed: Persian olives

Serke: vinegar

Sib: apples

Sir: garlic

Somaqh: sumac

The haft-sin spread also included a mirror, candles, painted eggs, a bowl of water with red goldfish, coins, hyacinth, traditional confectioneries, and the Quran.

Father and Mother always hallowed this ancient national occasion by reading verses from the Quran. While they prayed fervently for our health and prosperity in the coming year, we children excitedly anticipated the onset of the new year with a countdown: 10, 9, 8...

> *"The curious years, each emerging from that which preceded it...,"*
>
> *~ From 'Leaves of Grass'*

The new year would suddenly be announced with a loud bang from the city center, followed by neighbors' loud cheers. Thus, two weeks of gay festivities would begin. Friends and relatives would start to show in scores. All spiffed up and dressed in their newest once-a-year, tailor-made suits, haute couture dresses, and shiny hand-made leather shoes, they would pour in to embrace us and wish us a happy new year. Father usually handed out crisp currency bills he had earlier placed in the Holy

Book. We, the young, were bestowed coins or bills by the elders who came to visit. The merriment of the holiday season permeated the air that was not the same any longer. It was a sweeter air, a more auspicious air, ushering in a jollier time.

Imprudent Adolescence

"...from childhood's hour I've not been as others were...I've not seen as others saw...I couldn't bring my passions from a common spring...from the same source I haven't taken my sorrow...I couldn't awaken my heart to joy at the same tone...& all I lov'd...I lov'd alone...,"

~ E.A. Poe

I started elementary school at the age of five when Mother was just promoted to a managerial position at the school she taught. I was in the second grade when, one day, Mother told me that the school board commissioner, a luminary, was planning to visit our school, and protocol called for the school to receive him with pomp and splendor. Everyone prepared with enthusiasm for a ceremonious welcome. Mother taught me a famous two verse ode, a couplet, to recite as soon as he stepped into our classroom,

> *The king of flower rose from the grass*
> *May he be welcomed by the pansy & pine*

I practiced daily until I had the couplet memorized by heart, hoping to leave a good impression on this "illustrious person." But as soon as I saw him, erect, square of shoulders, with knotted eyebrows, step into our classroom, I was suddenly overtaken by a paralyzing panic attack. My mouth dried out, I lost my bearings, and could not utter a single audible word. I knew I had embarrassed my mother and deserved punishment, but she never scolded me for my unexpected, shameful faux pas. She never even mentioned it afterward.

Mother was inordinately wise, understanding, and gifted with a wide breadth of view. Her child-rearing was way ahead of her time. She never raised her hand on us, which taught us to eschew violence and never raise our hands on our children.

We lived in Fasa through my third grade. There, I recall a distant relative, an army officer who had just been transferred there, living with his old mother. I once saw him arrive home riding on a beautiful white horse, and that one glance changed my life for-ever.

I immediately fell in love with the way he majestically rode in that resplendent, badged uniform, the way he, glove in hand, pulled the rein, and the way he dismounted confidently like a chevalier in an early morning dream.

Many a time, I went and waited outside their house, just to see him arrive, and wide-eyed with eagerness, followed his every move. Then I would return home, ecstatic and content while my young imagination roamed wildly, depriving me of sleep.

We returned to Shiraz, and I attended school through the sixth grade where mother taught. I was different from other girls, and I felt it too. I often acted like a grown-up. In lieu of shrieking and playing raucously with other girls in the playground, I would quietly knit a blouse for Fataneh or a jacket for myself in the office during the breaks.

The teachers were surprised by my diligence and dexterity in knitting. They were amazed at how I was able to instinctively grasp proportions and measures when knitting. They also knew I had an affinity for baking. They thought it peculiar for a six-year-old to prefer knitting and baking to playing outside. Other girls regarded me with awe and respect when they saw me accompanied by my mother, a highly respected teacher.

Early on, I noticed that I was different from my schoolmates in many ways. Besides acting like an adult, I was simple, modest, and devoid of devices. I found other girls my age to be diabolic and scheming. Deceit and especially lying had always been anathema to me. I could never abide by dishonesty and still see myself as overly trusting. I guess that may be why I have often been taken advantage of by the mendacious type. Nevertheless, I have always been proud to say nothing but the inexorable truth, no matter what the consequences may hold.

***

"Tell a lie & the world is made of glass...,"

~ R. W. Emerson

It was finally time for high school, a momentous event in my life. In high school, my mother was not with me any longer, nor were the teachers, whom I had come to befriend, love, and rely upon. I was lost in a sea of girls, whom I thought wayward and conniving. There, I felt naked, lonely, and forlorn. To top it off, rain or shine, I had to walk alone a long way to reach school. On the way to and from school, I was often accosted by boys, who blurted crude jibes at me that filled my eyes with tears by the time I reached home, exhausted.

Shiraz was larger than Fasa and much different too. Going to school there seemed torturous to me. I could not despise it more. Unlike Fasa, in Shiraz, I was a mere speck in the multitude of girls in high school, and no one paid much attention to me.

I would notice girls congregating in groups of all sizes, whispering horrid secrets. They talked about the crushes they'd had on the male teachers, whom they were planning to romance, or they talked about the boys they had met on the way home, whom they were going to covertly meet again. It struck me as if they were not much of neophytes in the game of love.

***

"These yearnings, why are they...?"

~ *From 'Leaves of Grass'*

It all seemed abhorrent to me. I kept my distance with them. I was not their type. They did not subscribe to the same values as I did. Sometimes, I wished I could quit school altogether to not witness such unseemly behavior. Perhaps I was too rigid, or perhaps I was not as gutsy as they were, I am not sure. But their impudent behavior and indelicate language was, I thought, beneath the way I was raised, and signaled, I believed, a moral decay.

The way they conducted themselves was so distasteful to me that it would impact my child-rearing in the years to come. When I had my first child, a girl, I impulsively tried to keep a vigilant eye on her. For instance, I would be in constant touch with her teachers so I could be apprised of her doings and be able to prevent her from falling into the same vile adolescent traps I witnessed first-hand those days. But times would prove differently...

Holy Matrimony

"Years hence...may dawn an age, more fortunate,
alas! than we, which without hardness will be sage &
gay without frivolity. Sons of the world, oh, speed
those years... but while we wait, allow our tears...!"

~ Matthew Arnold

Even at a young age, I had many suitors. But my parents did not approve any of them, and citing my young age, would brush them all aside. In the middle of the school year when I had lost interest in school, even contemplating dropping out, something unexpected happened.

One day, our distant relative, the same army officer whom I had gone to see on countless afternoons riding his horse home, accompanied by his old mother and aunts, paid my parents a visit. Even though I was still awfully young to marry, they came to formally propose to me, of course through my parents.

Having already been fascinated by this man's aura and by his towering figure covered with dazzling military insignia, on top of the fact that marriage could now afford me a legitimate excuse to quit school altogether, the prospect of marriage seemed all the more appealing to me. Having already known my suitor's family well, my parents were also inclined to approve him.

The visits, intended to court and impress my parents, continued a few more times as was customary. I was not consulted on the matter though because, at thirteen years of age, I was assumed to have no standing in imparting a sound opinion. Custom at the time sufficed it with my parents consenting to my marriage.

Mother, an educated teacher and more progressive than her peers, however, broke the tradition and chose to ask my opinion. The suitor was

49

about my father's age, some eighteen years older than me. I, who was impatiently waiting for an excuse to mothball school and shun its hassles, not realizing the enormous consequences that would follow, lost no time in impetuously giving Mother my consent.

I did not have the dimmest inkling of the troubles, heartaches, and discordances this odd and disproportionate marriage would one day entail. At that young age, I was still out of step with reality and had not experienced life as a mature bride should.

At the time, though, I had other suitors who lived and studied in America, but my parents would not approve of them. Perhaps they thought once I left the country, they would never see me again.

With that unexpected marriage proposal, I became the center of attention overnight, and in an innocent, childlike way, enjoyed it too. Wherever we went, all eyes were fixed on me with unprecedented curiosity. Relatives and friends began observing my every move with interest abound.

The suitor's family lavished me with a trove of gifts, including a gold wedding ring, which was exceptionally titillating. I guess as a child, I must have regarded those knick-knacks as toys to play with. Imbued with childish joy and enthusiasm, I was literally lured into a malignant wedlock. I had received so many presents, I did not know which one to play with. I was naively oblivious to what the future might hold for me in this odd and hasty marriage.

True, Mother consented, but in retrospect, I can only attribute her consent to one thing. She was aware and hurt by Father's occasional forays into debauchery, which was not uncommon in that patriarchal society, but had hoped that my suitor, having been much older than me and past his running around, would not follow in Father's footsteps. She hoped the groom would be mature, family-oriented, and intent on taking care of his young and inexperienced bride. Sadly, she proved wrong in all of her assumptions.

Mother started preparing for my wedding with unprecedented excitement. Among other things, the preparation included sending out invites to a great many guests, shopping for *jahizieh* (dowry), planning the ceremonies, recruiting help, baking the confectioneries, and choosing a wedding gown for me.

Traditional marriages in Iran called for the bride to, through her family, procure all or most of the household items that were needed to start a life, known as jahizieh – a concept dating back to the times of the Babylonians – "intending to offer a bride as much lifetime security as her family could afford." During those times, I recall that it had become customary for the groom to provide a place for the couple to live in and for the bride to provide the jahizieh, the extent of which varied from family to family. The richer the family the more jahizieh the bride brought with her into the marriage and consequently the more favored, in the eyes of the groom's family, the bride became; and by implication, vis-à-vis the groom and his family, the more clout she would have. Those brides who could not afford a decent jahizieh were usually looked down on by the groom's family. Jahizieh was in a way meant to reciprocate the dower that the groom pledged to the bride. Dower was an amount usually in gold coins that, in case a marriage ended up in a divorce, the groom pledged to pay the bride. Dower was often subject to discussion and even negotiation between the two families when a marriage proposal was proffered. And not a few times those negotiations had turned into heated discussions and cause for cancelling a wedding.

One day, I innocently asked my mother if I could prop up my breast so that my wedding gown would look good on me. She expressed her objection in no uncertain terms.

"No, you must never pretend to be someone you're not. Everyone knows you're too young to have breasts. Besides, it won't look natural. You'll look ridiculous," she responded, chiding me.

Legal marriage at my young age required an official judiciary sanction. Before a sanction was issued, to make certain that a young bride was fit to marry, she had to be presented in person before a judiciary officer to be physically inspected. The officer took only one glance at the bride and, based on mere physical appearances, which probably included the makings of a woman, approved or disapproved of the marriage.

Incidentally, birth certificates lacked pictures those days.

To seal the judiciary's consent, my fiancé, Shahrokh, slipped his cousin, an older girl, in my stead. Once she, who was some eighteen years of age and gifted with more pronounced womanly proportions, was presented, the marriage was quickly approved. Retrospectively, I believe what he did was perhaps more than insidious. It was not much less than a heinous crime. My parents would never be privy to his brazen trickery.

The wedding was lavish and glittery in the extreme. It took place in our house on a mild winter night. The courtyard was covered, end to end, with oversized rugs. A score of bright kerosene lamps standing on tall posts copiously lighted the courtyard and the outside alley.

Tables of eight were set up, topped with round trays, filled with a variety of seasonal fruits and freshly baked confectioneries of different kinds.

An extravagant dinner, consisting of sumptuous dishes, was prepared by hired chefs.

The news of my wedding had spread like a wildfire in town, where many people knew us. In addition to the multitude of invited guests, a throng of curious locals appeared uninvited just for the sake of taking a quick peep at the "young beautiful bride," as they put it.

All went well, the night wore on, the ceremonies finally came to an end, and I went to the groom's house that night.

I was taught that a bride should enter the groom's house wearing a white wedding gown and should leave wearing a white burial shroud. I liked my husband when we married, and I was prepared to adhere to that traditional matrimonial maxim and even more.

"To have and to hold, from this day forward, for better, for worse, for richer, for poorer, in sickness and in health, to love and to cherish, till death do us part, according to God's holy ordinance; and thereto I pledge myself to you..."

Unfortunately, from the onset of my wedding that would turn out to be not much less than a tragic event for me, and even some time before the wedding, my in-laws began to see me in an antagonistic light, wasting no time to strike the first discordant notes. With every chance they were afforded, they denigrated me with an avalanche of saucy remarks.

In the hope of mollifying them, my parents kept turning a deaf ear to their oblique and disparaging comments and refused to react in kind. I guess they eschewed conflict because they knew their young loved one would be at the mercy of the groom and his family. Therefore, they were wary of reciprocal retaliation and, wishing to foster a congenial marital atmosphere for me, they chose placation over friction.

My Most Horrid Recollection

"Alas! everything is an abyss, action, dream, desire, speech...!"

~ Charles Baudelaire

If I was ever to be asked,

"What is the worst recollection of your past?"

I would not hesitate a moment to reply,

"My wedding night."

It was a terrible night, unlike any other I had ever experienced. After the ceremonies came to a close, we spent that night in a small, uncomfortable room, not covering much more than our bed, on top of a roof overlooking the bustling kitchen of a bakery shop below. With the new year approaching, that darned kitchen was busy with a large rowdy crew, baking through the night, working nonstop to the early hours of the morning.

Workers yelling and utensils banging were heard all night long with no let-up. The harsh noise had created an indescribably frightful backdrop on what was supposed to be a very special and romantic night for me.

That night would even turn for the worse when Shahrokh, conveniently and unceremoniously, rolled over and fell asleep, snoring loudly through the night. It must have seemed just another ordinary night for him with no special significance. But for me, it was a once-in-a-lifetime wedding night, an immensely special night, which turned out to be an unforgettably harrowing night.

I wished I could escape that doomed room, that torture chamber, but was afraid of falling off the roof in the pitch dark outside.

That ominous night was fittingly the harbinger of my gloomy marital life. Finally, the sky paled and the night came to an end after what seemed like an eternity, but a troublesome life followed soon after that would shatter all my sanguine hopes and expectations, foiling my aspirations, dashing my nascent spirits.

My mother-in-law was called Bi Bi and my sister-in-law was named Salar. She had a daughter named Soroor. After we were married, from the very first day, my in-laws turned into my arch-foes and formed an implacable, hostile alliance against me. Their attitude toward their innocent and inexperienced thirteen-year-old bride was laden with taunting, bickering, and complaining.

I, who was raised in a calm and affable setting thus far, bereft of chicanery and tension, was at a loss in dealing with my new antagonists. I did not know how to fend off their barrage of attacks. I was taught to always respect my elders and to never talk back. Their stinging sarcasm and incessant interference in my affairs started a dark chapter in my life, sinking my spirits to an all-time low.

As an example of their interference from the start, I have no wedding pictures, only because my envious sister-in-law, Salar, did not condone taking wedding pictures. After she had lost her husband in an auto accident, she was left with a girl and six boys to raise on her own. And they all ended up cooped up with my mother-in-law, my husband, and me under one roof. Soroor, the eldest child, was an elementary school teacher and the sole breadwinner for the family.

Three of the boys were my age. It did not take long for the two older boys to join my sworn enemies for no rhyme or reason either, rubbing more salt in my wound, helping the rest in throwing a salvo of insults and sniping comments at me. I pleaded with God,

"Dear Lord, is this what holy marriage is all about? How many more than my husband am I to be subservient to?"

By and by, I discovered the root cause of their deep-seated acrimony. It was none other than their despite for having a newcomer share Shahrokh's income, which they did not like. They expected his continued financial support with no impediments, and feared losing it. They saw me as cramping their lifestyles. Simply put, I was one more mouth to feed, and they did not like it.

***

"My life is not an apology, but a life...,"

~ R. W. Emerson

Therefore, they regarded me as their nemesis. They continued in their vile ways, depriving me of peace. For instance, I could not even buy a pair of shoes without their consent. Sadly, my husband could not have cared less and made no efforts to support me or ameliorate the tense situation. The notion of love in marriage seemed to be alien to him.

Often, when he arrived home from work, instead of spending time with me, his new bride, he was snatched by his sister into a corner where, shrouded in secrecy, they whispered endlessly. I once asked,

"What was it that you all talked about for so long?"

Smothering my feelings, he returned bitterly with a frown,

"It is not your business to know. It is her personal affairs."

Later, I would learn that she was hitting Shahrokh up for money.

I endured it all, a torrent of abuse with no end in sight. I endured because I believed I was destined to be tied to this family. Therefore, instead of rebellion, I chose self-mortification and servile obedience to that encyclopedia of human folly, hoping for a happy-as-can-be life following the prevailing "Chekhovian gloom."

Our house was a good distance away from where my parents lived. I did not see them from month to month. Telephone was not commonly available, and one had to go afoot from place to place to visit someone. I would tell Shahrokh that I missed my family and wanted to see them, but he was either exhausted from working or had other engagements planned and could not take me to visit them. I was under the impression that this was what married life was all about and one had to take it as it was.

***

"Blessed are the meek, for they shall inherit the earth...,"

~ Matthew

Shopping for groceries was another ordeal unto itself. What was bought depended on what the boys felt like having, and everyone else had to cave in because the boys came first. Ironically, I had soon gotten used to the boys, and since we were all about the same age, I began to see and love them like my own brothers and willingly catered to their wishes.

When we traveled, which was not often, we rode on a dilapidated, squeaky bus in the dust and heat, and like a flotilla, the whole family would be in tow. Anywhere we went, Salar was always first in line and ahead of me. Shahrokh never sat next to me on the bus, which made me feel slighted. Instead, I had to sit next to Salar, my antagonist and the perennial thorn in my side.

At times, I fell asleep on the bus, and unknowingly rested my head on Salar's shoulder instead of my husband's. I wished my husband sat next to me, so I could cozy up to him, snuggle, and rest my head on his strong shoulder and savor him like a woman should savor her husband.

I, at the ages of 13 and 14, perhaps habitually, had come to love my husband, yet sensed a dismal vacuum due to the stark indifference by him. He never made the slightest attempt to change his ways and failed to nurture me with love. I was treated unfairly, I knew, but had no choice except to swallow my pride and put up with what life had in store for me.

***

"When Love loves Love for its own sake, when the self is dead, we shall meet Him...,"

~ Sufi Chant

Freedom at Last

"From this hour, freedom! From this hour I ordain myself loos'd of limits & imaginary lines...,"

~ Walt Whitman

"The smallest worm will turn, being trodden on...,"

~ From 'King Henry'

A long time passed, and one day when I was visiting my parents, I confided to them about my despicable marital life, my in-laws' cruel behavior, relentless interference, and grueling mistreatment. My parents were deeply saddened and distressed by what they heard. When Shahrokh came after me that night, my mother interceded angrily,

"I won't let you take my daughter back to that hellish house with your clannish lifestyle. This is not a life she deserves. My daughter is being tortured and taken advantage of in your home. This is no living. She deserves better."

After much arguing, he returned flustered without me that night.

A short time later, Shahrokh, having finally gotten tired of his family's obnoxious behavior that constantly resulted in tension and a corrosive living atmosphere, in a surprising act of about-face, came to the understanding that he, too, was fed up with all the family feuds and could not stand it anymore.

He, at last, realized that our home was no Garden of Eden and volunteered to rent a separate house for the two of us in the proximity of my parents.

We made the move, marking the beginning of our marital life

independent of his family, in a toxic-free environment. Bi Bi clung to us, though, which was more bearable than living with the whole bunch of them.

By degrees, we started to live a more normal life, free of intrusion and turmoil. This would not, in any way, diminish my in-laws' stinging, oblique comments from afar. Liberated, we began to enjoy our budding life together. We started to socialize with Shahrokh's friends and peers and began to live a life like a married couple should, in our new house, which felt akin to a fortress for me.

Shahrokh's friends could not believe I was his wife when they first met me. And when they were assured that I was indeed his wife, they thought I must be his second or third wife! Until I had my first child, Setareh, wherever I went, folks thought I was single and contemplated proposing to me on behalf of a brother or a cousin! And this continued on after I had my first child, a girl. After I became a mother, I would often joke,

"Who are you talking about? Me or my daughter?"

I guess I was gifted with beauty but was oblivious to it, and it did not much cross my mind. I was simple, naïve, and never learned the essentials of coquetry, not even with my husband. Nor did he, bereft of the slightest amorous disposition, know how to enamor a wife, which would leave an everlasting void in my mature life.

After we settled in our new house, my husband's relatives began to see me in a different light. Suddenly, they began seeking my counsel on different matters. For instance, they would ask my advice regarding their weddings.

They would ask my opinion on the bride's gown, makeup, and even food and settings. They began to value my taste and opinion, for they knew I had a keen interest in fashion, makeup, and interior design, in which I would later pursue a career.

***

"A fig tree looking upon a fig tree becometh fruitful...,"

~ Arabic Proverb

No Man's Land

"I went to the woods...to see if I couldn't learn what it had to teach & not, when I came to die, discover that I hadn't lived...."

~ Henry D. Thoreau

Before long, Shahrokh was given a new assignment and was transferred to Bushehr, some 288 kilometers driving distance southwest of Shiraz; a city with an arid desert climate, lying in a vast plain, running along the coastal region of the Persian Gulf.

Bushehr had existed since the Greek Macedonian Seleucid dynasty in 300 B.C. Later, it was one of the main seaports of the Sassanian navy, and it was named after the first king of that dynasty.

It had been a major trade center in the past few centuries. In the 18th century, the British India Company had built a trading post there, establishing it as a prominent commercial port. It had been occupied by the British army—first during the Anglo-Persian war of the late 19th century—and later during World War I.

Shortly after my husband was transferred there, my mother-in-law, our army appointed servant, and I joined him there. We settled in an old house on the verge of a scorching desert, in the middle of nowhere. The house was raised a good way from the ground, and we had to climb a score of steps to reach a long, dark, and narrow corridor that connected four widely separated bedrooms, two on each side, forming an island in the middle, which was conveniently used as our living area.

The weather was blistering hot, and by keeping the bedroom windows open day and night, the air rushed in from four sides, which only mildly cooled the sitting area and made it barely tolerable to lounge in. We had no running water, nor a refrigerator. An outside pool was dug to collect rainwater that was then poured into many terra-cotta clay jars. Those jars were used to filter the impure rainwater into quasi-drinking-water. That same water was heated on a wood-burning stove for bathing.

We lived a simple provincial life, devoid of amenities.

Not far from us was a mud hut settlement of three families, all brothers, who lived with their wives and children. The wives accompanied their husbands to their nearby ranch every day, where they tilled the earth with oxen. I often walked there and watched them with curious eyes. They were happily working nonstop, goading oxen, sowing, planting, fertilizing, and watering all day long. They stayed in mud houses and lived on bread and dates and sometimes fish. The bread was made in a mud baking oven.

I was curious as to why they ate dates in such hot weather. I was later told that they had to eat dates to raise their body temperatures to above the outside temperature to cool off.

They began the day with a generous pinch of tobacco tucked securely behind their lower lips, then off to work they went. They raised chicken and cattle and made yogurt, buttermilk, butter, and cheese—and planted leafy vegetables, eggplants, legumes, and melons.

They struck me as affable and peaceful, never arguing, quarreling, or raising their voices. They worked collectively and in perfect unison without a hitch, children helping too. At times, they blurted English words, such as "Tomato" and "Hi." Using English words must have been a result of the British influence when Britain had ruled there at one time. We were often invited to their mud houses, and they were spellbound with awe when Shahrokh spoke with the aura of an army commander. They regarded him with deference.

A few kilometers away stood erect a building that had at one time been built by the British army and later turned into the fortified headquarters of the Iranian Imperial Army. The army commander and his family resided there. The building was superlatively luxurious with full amenities, such as running water, water heater, bathrooms, air conditioning, and refrigerators. It also featured tennis courts and stables. It could have been a resort out of Palm Springs, California.

Shahrokh worked in that complex. An army jeep arrived each morning to drive him to work. That jeep was our only mode of transportation. It also took us to town to shop for provisions. Since air-conditioned cars did not exist, and the heat was unbearable, the favored means of transportation was the topless jeep, which was all that was seen on those hot, dusty, and narrow roads, looking from a distance like little specks moving about in the hazy, scorching horizon.

Interestingly, at the time, a colleague and friend of my husband, also an army officer and a good looking one, began to show an amorous interest in me! His wife, some years older than him, was bereft of good looks with age. With every excuse he could muster, he came to visit us. He flew from Shiraz in a small army plane, which always descended once it neared our house, and as it flew over our house, he would throw his hat to me as a gesture of...?! I would then pick it up and call Shahrokh on a walkie talkie, announcing his arrival.

They came home together after work. Shahrokh never made much of him throwing me his hat. He either did not care or else he was too trusting; I was not certain. But I made every effort to conduct myself in a scrupulous way to avoid showing any hints of reciprocating his affectionate proclivities. He still came to Bushehr often and stayed for the night.

After dinner, he usually asked to play cards, which lasted till late into the night. While he had a meaningful smile, mischievously playing on his lips, I would notice him showering me with his furtive, admiring glances. He would not be the last of Shahrokh's friends who coveted me.

To escape the sweltering heat at night, we had to sleep on the outside balcony. As night fell, foxes crept in to pounce on our neighbor's chickens, and soon mayhem would ensue. Sometimes, foxes even stealthily slipped onto our own balcony, lounging close to our bed, staring at us, showing their white teeth. I now wonder,

"How did we dare live in such wild and unsafe surroundings, such unruly wilderness, such uncongenial country?"

My husband could not care less, I was sure.

Soror, my sister-in-law's daughter, paid us a visit once and wasted no time in stoking the fire of a quarrel between Shahrokh and me. Never was I immune to her insidious behavior until she remarried. She always created maelstroms in my life, sowing the seeds of discord any chance she got, any way she could.

Brother's Loss, Return to Shiraz, & Motherhood

"O, death, where is thy sting? O grave, where is thy victory...?"

~ Corinthians

"Pale death beats equally at the poor man's gate & the palaces of kings...,"

~ Horace

"From my rotting body, flowers shall grow, I'm in them & that's eternity...,"

~ Edvard Munch.

My father had to spend a few months in Lar on a government assignment. It has been said that Lar, a tiny city, some 300 kilometers southeast of Shiraz, had been named after the first settler there.

It had been a major stopping point along the route to the Persian Gulf in the 17th century. That old city was famous for having the Bazaar of Qausariye, a pre-Safavid dynasty creation, and a UNESCO World Heritage site.

Lar had also been the name of a famous hero in Shahnameh, the book of the Persian national epic poems, the longest of its kind in the world, written in the 10th century by the famous Persian poet Ferdowsi.

Although Father's sojourn in Lar would have been no more than a few months, not knowing what lay in wait for her, mother took her three children, including her newborn girl, Firoozeh, and went with him.

Tragedy struck ruthlessly and my younger brother, Fatah, only 7 years old, was stricken with a bad case of jaundice in Lar. Due to the lack of modern medicine, he could not be cured and died there. His unexpected death dealt an irreparable blow to our collective psyche. We were simply devastated. It was a huge loss for our family.

***

"Then shall the dust return to the earth as it was &
the spirit shall return onto God who gave it...,"

~ Ecclesiastes.

He was buried there. And immensely heavy-hearted and despondent, barely able to bear the burden of that grave calamity, my parents returned without their son.

May his sweet soul rest in peace.

"O love, be moderate, allay thy ecstasy, in measure
rain thy joy, scant this excess! I feel too much thy
blessing... make it less, for fear I surfeit...,"

~ Shakespeare

Once Shahrokh's assignment in Bushehr ended, we moved back to Shiraz and lived with my parents for a short time before renting a house.

During those days, I do not know why I could not wait to be a mother and have children of my own. People mocked me, saying,

"You are still a child yourself. Why do you want a child?"

In retrospect, I think I wanted a child to fill the void created in my life by my husband as a result of his "sins of omissions and commissions." He was not in the least affectionate. I received no love from him; love that is the main pillar of a happy marriage; love that is needed to sustain a happy marriage. I was deprived of that most heavenly bliss.

Finally, when I was 16, Setareh was born. I gave birth to her in Merselin, the hospital of choice for the upper crust in Shiraz. The first time I laid my eyes on her and met her dark eyes, my whole body trembled with ecstasy, and I felt love with every fiber of my being. I finally discovered and was discovered by love. It was a miracle, no less, a celestial bliss. And I at last felt surfeit of love.

My husband had kept wishing for a boy during my pregnancy and did not hesitate to say so either. I was worried that a girl would dash his hopes. But it took only one glance at our newborn for him to love her, just the same. It was my baby who, for the first time in my life, reciprocated my love, nurtured me with love, and saved me with love. Two years hence, I bore a son, Sadra, and a year later, another son, Arash.

Sizdebedar Outing Incident

"O Sword, you're the younger brother, the latter-
born, your triumph, however exultant, must one day
be over, in the beginning, was the word...,"

~ *Hilda Doolittle*

Before Sadra was born, an unexpected and frightful incident occurred that forever left its indelible, ill-omened imprint on my mind. One year on *Sizdebedar*, the thirteenth day of the first month of the new year following Nowruz, the once-a-year occasion for the Iranian traditional outing, going back many millennia, my husband decided to invite a large number of family and friends to camp at a serene spot in the untouched countryside near a village by the name of Panir Banoo.

Sizdebedar is an Iranian outing festival held annually on the thirteenth day of *farvardin*, the first month of the Iranian calendar, during which people spend time picnicking outdoors in a park or in the countryside. It was believed that joy and laughter clean the mind from all evil thoughts, and a picnic is usually a festive, happy event. *Sizdah* means thirteen, and *bedar*, means to get rid of; hence, getting rid of thirteen. Since ancient times, Iranians have enjoyed this day that marks the end of the Nowruz celebrations. The first twelve days of the year are said to symbolize order in the world and in the lives of people. The thirteenth day marks the beginning of the return to ordinary daily life.

Sizdebedar had been known to be a day to ask for rain. In ancient Iran, every day had been called by a different name and belonged to a different Zoroastrian deity known as *yazat*. This day had been devoted to the deity rain known as *tir*. This day is also the Iranian version of the prank-playing April Fools' Day. It corresponds to the second day of April. Pranks have been played on this holiday since the times of the Achaemenid Empire, some 500 years B.C.

A ritual performed at the end of this picnic day is to throw away the grass blades known as *sabzeh* that had been grown in a dish and set on the haft-sin spread during the new year. The sabzeh is supposed to have collected all the sickness, pain, and ill fate that could have befallen the family throughout the coming year.

Another tradition on this day is the knotting of blades of grass by unmarried girls in the hope of finding a companion. The knotting of the grass blades represents love and the bondage of a man and a woman.

The year of the incident, all of us, young and old, started preparation days in advance with excitement for this event. A variety of scrumptious foods were prepared in large pots, to be warmed for lunch. Other provisions, such as fruit, melons, sweets, bread, cheese, and preserves were also tucked away in picnic baskets.

In the early, grey hours of that infamous morning, when the air was still fraught with the haze of dawn, we drove door to door in a large army transport vehicle to pick up some of the 50 or so invited attendees. Others had decided to bring their own cars.

We decamped at a pristine location, where trees were blooming in the inebriating spring air, and the clear, cold water was lazily bathing the dazzling pebbles in a brook. We started to boil water for tea and began frying eggs for breakfast. We also started to warm up the saffron rice, lamb, and chicken stew that we had prepared for lunch. We kept the melons in the cold brook water to chill.

Just as we were about to start eating breakfast, we noticed one of our youngsters squabbling with a local youth. Men had gathered around the two to intercede. Suddenly, on nearby hilltops overlooking our camp, a herd-like drove of locals, who were members of a nomadic tribe (either the Qashqai, Boirahmadi, or Ilkhani) appeared against the rising sun.

At the sound of what seemed like a whistle, they descended on us, running wildly, much like an invading army, brandishing sticks and chains in the air. They began to attack and beat us indiscriminately when they reached us. We were screaming and running away in every direction, haplessly trying to fend off blows from the left and the right.

Some of those who had brought their cars attempted to flee the melee, but their efforts were to no avail. All the automobiles and even the army truck had already been covertly dismantled in anticipation of our flight. It felt like a scene out of a horror movie. We were puzzled as to how and when they were able to pull such a surreptitious stunt on us. All the while, the belligerents were chanting a warlike song, yelling insults, beating us with no let-up, and would not listen to our repeated pleas.

The fracas lasted a long time. Pots of rice and stew were overturned, and supplies were scattered everywhere, creating a thoroughly littered scene. All I managed to do was to tightly clutch my newborn in my arms to protect her from the rampant blows, which proved to be not an easy task. I had never before in my life seen such pugnacious behavior by a group of people.

***

> *"O, withered is the garland of the war, the soldier's pole is fallen...,"*
>
> *~ Shakespeare*

Shahrokh, like all the other army officers, was in possession of a pistol, which he happened to have on him on that day. Suddenly, intending to break the fight, he pulled out his pistol and started shooting in the air. An awed hush fell for a few short seconds. Then the mayhem resumed, and worse yet, loud cries were heard,

"Who did that? Someone has been shot. Someone has been murdered. We will kill the shooter. Who was it? You have killed one of us. We want revenge."

Apparently, Shahrokh, lost among the large crowd, had not been seen shooting his pistol. When no one claimed to had been the shooter, the villains approached us, the women and the children, crying for revenge,

"If he doesn't show his face, we'll kill his wife and children. Which one of you is his wife? Where are his children?"

I was frightened to the bone. All I managed to do was to keep my daughter pressed against me and keep quiet, all the while shaking all over.

This went on for some time until, miraculously, a young member of our group was able to slip away and reach the army quarters in Shiraz, recounting our precarious plight. Once the army officers were informed that Shahrokh, a well-known colonel, and his family were in grave danger, they lost no time in sending an army convoy to deliver us from the vicious claws of those bloodthirsty nomads.

The missing auto parts were recovered and we at long last, driving closely behind army vehicles that were escorting us for protection, started for home in a convoy. We looked much like a defeated army, beaten, exhausted, and famished. We had not driven far before we came upon a large hole in the middle of the narrow road that had rendered the road impassable. That hole must have been dug by the same locals to impede our flight. Soldiers quickly dismounted, took out their shovels, and filled the hole. We were later told that they had planned to keep us there through the night so they could slit our throats. That doomed day was perhaps the most frightful and taxing day of our lives.

Word had meanwhile spread in Shiraz that a group of intruding campers had been murdered in Pir Banoo. People who knew us came worried the next day to make sure we were unharmed. After that cruel mistreatment, we were shocked and dejected for days. I had never before witnessed such a horrifying incident. Days passed and news arrived that the village elder (de facto chieftain), known as the kadkhoda, had been held accountable and severely upbraided by the authorities. To this day, the horrid memories of that unforgettable incident send chills down my spine.

We later realized, on that infamous day, the members of that nomadic tribe had been roaming about in the proximity of our campsite – their livestock grazing on the budding spring pasture. These tribes consisted mostly of Turkic, nomadic pastoralists one would find in the countryside near the city of Shiraz around that time of the year. They would travel with their flocks twice yearly between the summer highland pastures north of Shiraz and the winter pastures on lower and warmer lands near the Persian Gulf, to the southwest of Shiraz. They were famous for being great warriors. And because of their inborn recalcitrance and separatist inclinations, taming and reining them in had been a constant challenge for the central government in Tehran. And on that infamous day, we had unluckily fallen prey to those exemplary warriors.

To Isfahan

"The thing is true, according to the law of the Medes & Persians which altereth not...,"

~Daniel 6:1

Sometime later, my husband was relocated to Isfahan, a city some 500 kilometers north of Shiraz by car, situated in the lush plains of the Zayanderud River, at the foothills of the Zagros Mountains, one of the largest cities the world had known at one time.

Isfahan is located at the intersection of the two, principal north-south and east-west routes that traverse Iran. Human habitation in the region traces back to the Paleolithic period.

In the 5th century, Queen Shushandukht, the Jewish consort of the Sassanid king Yazdegerd I, had settled a colony of Jews there.

But Isfahan had first flourished in the 11th century during the Turkic Seljuq dynasty and again in the 17th century during the Persian Safavid dynasty as its glorious capital under Shah Abbas, ushering in a golden age for the city, and with its famous grand boulevards, tiled mosques and minarets, palaces, and bridges, turning it to one of the largest and most beautiful cities in the known world.

After having been subjected to inhumane mistreatments, migrants from the Caucasus and Armenian communities had poured into the city, adding to its cosmopolitan diversity, creating one of the world's oldest and largest Armenian quarters in the Julfa district of Isfahan, which hosts the notable Vank Cathedral.

The Naghsh-e-Jahan Square, a world heritage site designated by UNESCO is still one of the largest city squares in the world. Little wonder, the phrase, "Isfahān-nesf-e-jahān," or "Isfahan, half of the world," was coined in praise of the city.

The Shaykh Bahai hammam, a historical bathhouse in Isfahan, is another wonder of that city. It belongs to the Safavid era. It was built in 1616 by Shaykh Bahai during the reign of Shah Abbas I. It is believed that this bathhouse can be warmed by only one lit candle under the cauldron of the stove.

Minar Jonban is yet another historical site to see in Isfahan. It is a mosque-like monument that was built in the 14th century during the Ilkhanate dynasty as a shrine for the tomb of a Sufi by the name of Amu Abdollah Soqla. Its notable feature is that if one of the minarets is shaken, the other minaret will shake as well. Tourists are invited to climb the stairs to the top of one of the minarets to shake it and to observe the shaking of the second minaret.

In Isfahan, we settled in a spacious and comfortable house. I was particularly happy that, unlike Shiraz, our new house did not have a pool. I guess having experienced the bitter taste of near-drowning early on, I was wary of a pool for my daughter's safety. But one day, I noticed she was missing. I looked inside the rooms but could not find her. I hurried to the courtyard. She was nowhere to be found. We had a front door as well as a back door in the courtyard. The back door opened onto a river bank. I noticed that it was open. I guessed she must have gone out through the back door. I frantically dashed out the back door and saw her trotting along the river! I was at once shaking and overcome with joy at the sight of her sprinting, so delightfully and so carefreely!

Shahrokh was put in command of the military police forces there, which was regarded as a highly touted position. He told me one day,

"Did you know that in this town, day workers start to gather in one spot at the crack of dawn, waiting to be picked up for day work? But oddly enough, Isfahanis choose only native laborers, and will not use non-Isfahanis, unless they have to, and will pay them only half as much if they do."

Unlike Shiraz, where there was an equal business opportunity for all, one seldom saw non-Isfahani proprietors or shopkeepers in Isfahan. Before long, I also noticed that the local shopkeepers charged non-natives more for the same goods they sold, such as groceries and fruits. To be treated fairly when shopping, I was advised by friends to utter my words in the local dialect.

While living in Isfahan, we frequented the main city theatre and enjoyed the theatrical performances by Arhame Sadr, a popular national satirist, at the cusp of his career at the time. He had a genius for wrapping current events, societal issues, and even politics, which were forbidden at the time, into finely spun satirical cocoons, starting a nuanced collective dialogue that people who yearned for democracy and an open society hungered for. With a finger on the nation's pulse, he had a good understanding of the pervading collective mood of the time.

There was also a notable fellow in Isfahan by the name of Yooz Bashi, who idly loitered all day along a well-known street named Charbagh, with nothing particular to do except to shower bystanders with hilarious jibes and taunts. He was widely liked and enjoyed by the locals and visitors alike. He had made a name for himself to almost a local legend, a "must-see" for the tourists, alongside other historical sites and monuments!

Paradoxically, Isfahan, that fairly large metropolis of historical significance, the one-time capital of the glorious Safavid dynasty which once stretched from Afghanistan to the North Caucasus, lacked a sewage system in those days. Human refuse was, instead, collected daily on donkeys with their jingling sounds filling the air as they languidly moved to dump their loads outside of the city.

The legend goes that one day, Yooz Bashi had been in the vicinity of the TBT bus terminal, where hordes of tourists disembarked daily. A newly arrived tourist had asked him,

"What are these donkeys carrying?"

He is known to have quickly quipped,

"Oh, nothing, just the newly arrived tourists!"

He was swift with a hilarious quip and an impromptu jibe, uttered in a serious tone. People deliberately approached him to ask a question and reveled in his mocking replies, cracking with laughter. He reminds me of the Iranian-born soup mogul Ali Yeganeh of Manhattan, also known as the "Soup Nazi," famously satirized in the sitcom *Seinfeld*.

The door-to-door beggars in Isfahan were notorious. They were well organized and resilient. They knocked on doors daily, asking for money. Our servant, a local also, told me one day,

"Ma'am; they are not poor. This is how they make money. They work and live in groups of seven to a dozen, one cooking and cleaning the house, the others working, with shifts rotating."

I then understood why they only asked for money and never for bread or food.

While in Isfahan, I recall an incident that involved an officer friend of Shahrokh's. His friend, a colonel also, had one day been busy cleaning his pistol when one of those persistent beggars had knocked on his door, accosting him for money. Pistol in hand, he had tried to close the door on the beggar. But the beggar had pushed on the door, incessantly pleading for money. Then for a quick second he had shown his pistol to the beggar, saying that he had been in the middle of cleaning his pistol and not able to give him any money. By mere bad luck, his pistol had inadvertently gone off, fatally shooting the beggar, an elderly woman.

Soon after that incident, a throng of locals had showed up, bent on exacting revenge. Shahrokh, for the safety of his friend, decided to incarcerate him in his own army quarters. Still, endless people kept on pouring into Shahrokh's quarters, claiming to be the victim's relatives, demanding to bring him to justice on their own.

After a few months of negotiating with the family members of the deceased beggar and many court appearances, Shahrokh was finally able to secure his friend's release by having him pay a large sum to the plaintiffs to obtain their consent in the lawsuit.

In retrospect, I found the natives of Isfahan to possess a unique sense of pride...pride in their history, pride in their past grandeur, pride in their culture, and pride in their dialect. Tightly knitted, they hung together and regarded the outsiders with wide suspicion.

Sister, Parvaneh - Wedding

*"We marry, a gentler scion to the wildest stock, &
conceive a bark of baser kind, by bud of nobler race.
This is an art, which does mend nature...the art itself
is nature...,"*

~ Shakespeare

When we lived in Isfahan, Parvaneh was proposed to by a young man from a noble family, and my parents accepted. As mentioned before, in those days, it was paramount for the bride's parents to approve the groom and his family.

Gladly, my husband was transferred back to Shiraz just in time for their engagement and the wedding ceremony that followed.

While a bliss of mammoth proportions, weddings in those days were tedious, cumbersome, and taxing. Much planning, preparation, and hard work was involved, such as selecting and buying jewelry, the bride's gown, clothes, and the jahizieh which included all household goods needed by a couple to start a new life.

There was also help to recruit, food to prepare, confectioneries to bake, seasonal fruits to buy, entertainment to plan for, and gifts to select. After they were married, for almost up to a year, the newlyweds were lavished with gifts.

The groom was of high birth; he was born and reared in a large, reputable, and established family in Shiraz. Their wedding has remained a nostalgic event for me to this day.

The groom's family owned a large house. On the right side lived a brother with his family. On the left side lived two unmarried sisters. On the back-side, in the middle, the newlyweds Parvaneh and Ardeshir began to live.

The gay festivities lasted seven days and seven nights. Family and friends feasted three times a day, breakfast, lunch, and dinner, on delectable and delicious foods that hired cooks had prepared and laid out.

As was customary, to add to the gaiety of the occasion, local itinerant musicians came unannounced to perform, and they were paid a shabash, an amount in currency bills. They performed enthusiastically, and the attendees danced to the music. Much mirth was in the air.

The groom's family, uniquely witty, further enlivened the ceremonies with their gay mood. It was a dazzling and unforgettable event.

Ardeshir turned out to be a great husband for Parvaneh. He has been kind, caring, and loyal. After they married, he warned his sisters to not ever mistreat his new bride, or else! He has been supportive of her throughout their married life, and that is probably why his folks have always regarded my sister with utmost respect. Thankfully, they are a happily married couple to this day.

Unfortunately, when I was pregnant with my second child, Sadra, Parvaneh suffered a perilous miscarriage. Her eight-month-old baby died in her womb. Although pregnant myself, I chose to stand by her side and take care of her during those critical days, which luckily ended up in a full recovery.

Later, she would give birth to a boy, Hamid, and two girls, Rakhshandeh and Tabandeh. Today, Hamid is a well-known physician, a heart specialist, and he has two sons of his own. One is an engineer, the other is studying to be a physician.

Rakhshandeh is a gynecologist, specializing in detecting ailing fetuses, in time to provide parents with an abortion option. Aside from being a practicing physician with a private office, she is also a hospital president. She is well known and highly revered in the medical community in Shiraz.

Parvaneh's second daughter, Tabandeh, married after high school. She is endowed with impeccable management skills, and she currently manages the family properties with unflagging devotion. She is the go-to person when the family is in a crunch. In a country still new to technology, she is surprisingly up to date with digital devices. When Facebook had just started, she called from Iran,

"Auntie, please download this site."

"Which site?"

"Facebook."

"What is that?"

"In Farsi it means, *ketabe soorat*, the book of the face."

Then she, in Iran, taught me, in America, all there was to know about Facebook. When in need of help in the digital domain, I still call her.

I had tried to persuade Parvaneh's children to migrate to America at a young age, but their father Ardeshir would not budge. He would say that they could not afford to leave Iran, because they owned too much property there, which had deeply embedded them in the old country.

The three children were bequeathed a large ranch, and when they decided to build their houses there, it was Tabandeh who took upon herself the cumbersome task of managing the construction, a herculean endeavor, no less, in a country like Iran with all its usual gender prejudices.

Tabandeh is, by nature, a habitual traveler. She has been to more countries in the seven continents around the globe than anyone could imagine. A couple of years ago, she led an unforgettable ten-day tour that took us all, including my daughter, my sister Firoozeh, her daughter, and myself to visit British Colombia's Vancouver. Tabandeh was accompanied by her wonderful husband and her daughter, a dentist. There, we all stayed in a sizable Airbnb Vacation Rental Home and rented a full-size sedan that took us sightseeing. It was the trip of a lifetime. Last year, in 2019, she led yet another tour, this time, destined for Quebec. In the

French-speaking city of Montreal, we also stayed in an Airbnb Vacation Rental Home with a breathtaking view of the Saint Lawrence River. This year, she was planning a trip to Spain, which was unfortunately canceled due to the pandemic.

Perfidy That Goes Unpunished

*"He draweth out the thread of his verbosity finer
than the staple of his argument...,"*

~ Shakespeare

When Parvaneh was pregnant with Rakhshandeh, she was admitted to the Merselin, the celebrated hospital in Shiraz. As per custom, the expectant mothers stayed in private rooms in the maternity ward of the hospital for 10 days. Those rooms that were to host a throng of visitors, who would arrive with gifts and flowers to congratulate the parents, were decorated to taste and fully supplied. Being her older sister, I saw it incumbent upon myself to keep her company in the hospital during that time.

One day, out of boredom and for sheer fun, I decided to pull a prank on Shahrokh. I was curious to find out how he was coping with my absence. When no one was around during lunchtime, I went to the hospital's office and called him. I changed the tone of my voice,

"Hi."

"Well, Hello. Who is this?"

"I'm someone you don't remember, but I have seen you somewhere."

"Oh, really? Have we met before?"

"No. Not formally. But I've seen you somewhere. You probably don't remember me, but I can never forget you. I think you are very handsome, and I think I got a crush on you, and wanna see you sometime."

"Well, well, mighty sweet of you. You have a nice voice yourself. I wouldn't mind seeing you either."

I suddenly went berserk. My blood froze. I oscillated between rage and laughter, not knowing whether to cry or to laugh. While flustered at how easily my husband could betray my trust, I decided to continue the prank calls for the remainder of the days I stayed in the hospital. But I kept asking myself,

"How could he, at his old age, married to me, a young wife, muster the courage and have the audacity to betray me so easily, schmoozing with a total stranger, and God knows what else? Has he no shame? Whatever happened to our holy wedding vow?"

"Many a fool, lantern in hand, search for the sun in the desert...," Rumi

I boiled with rage when he one day said,

"I'll let you in on a little secret, just between the two of us. Did you know that I look forward to talking to you at this time every day? Your voice is awfully soothing. It relaxes me and I think I've gotten used to it. I don't know what I'll do without you."

That almost killed me.

Since Parvaneh was scheduled to be released the following day, I proposed to see him then.

"Honey, I'm dying to see you. Why don't we meet tomorrow at 5 o'clock in the afternoon, across from Mayak Movie Theatres?

"You got it. It's a date. I've been waiting for this. I just don't know how I can wait that long."

After Parvaneh was discharged from the hospital the next day, I returned home and waited for Shahrokh to arrive from work. He arrived home at 3 o'clock in the afternoon. He showered, shaved, dressed in his newest suit, and splashed a copious amount of cologne on himself.

"Where to honey?" demanded I.

"Oh, nowhere, just another boring, work-related meeting," he returned laconically.

"At Mayak Theatres?"

"What're you talking about? Why do you say that?" he answered with a flushed face.

"The gal you were gonna meet is standing right in front of you."

With embarrassment sinking in, blood rushed to his face, laying bare his blatant dishonesty. At the same time, having had his amorous aspirations foiled, he rankled to the core with disappointment and turned livid. But still unfazed, he tried to bridle his temper with an effort and belied the manifest truth. He simply denied the whole saga.

***

"Speak the truth & all things are vouchers & the very roots of the grass underground do seem to stir to bear you witness...,"

~ *R. W. Emerson*

For a moment, I wondered wistfully how disloyal men can be. A recurring question kept pestering me: How can a man, who is already in a binding marriage, deprive his wife of love and attention, and instead, entertain amorous thoughts, wooing a complete stranger, and without any qualms fall into a love trap so easily?

A face-off and much arguing, bickering, and wrangling followed that revealing incident. He continued to brazenly deny the whole thing, claiming he knew it was me all along, but only for sheer fun decided to go along with the prank.

I thought, "What a big lie, and as dumb as the day is long."

If he knew, then why did he spiff up to go see his date? Why did he not say he recognized my voice?

Despite the newly created mistrust, I bore the brunt, took the high road, chose acquiescence, stayed in the marriage, and did not let that incident jaundice my view of our relationship, because I was a mother after all. I had to stay in the game, I thought, and I had to try to piece together an undeniably shattered marriage, a marriage scant of love and justice. Could this be called anything less than a titanic sacrifice?

First House

"Flow, flow the waves hated, accursed, adored, the waves of mutation...no anchorage is...,"

~ *R. W. Emerson*

"Set thine house in order...,"

~*Isaiah*

A few years into our marriage, I craved for a house of our own. My marriage had taught me that to accomplish anything of significance or acquire anything of substance in my life, I had to take action alone and could not rely on my husband when it came to important decisions.

I wanted a house, but Shahrokh was dead-set against it; instead, he wanted a horse. He loved horses and, endowed with exceptional horsemanship, he had a knack for equestrian sports. He won in national competitions in dressage, cross-country, and show jumping. Whenever he competed, family and friends usually gathered to cheer him on. For me though, those joyful moments were only transient. I wanted a house of our own that would be a permanent bliss.

My family and friends were all supportive of me in my quest for a house, but Shahrokh could not care less. Finally, when I realized that my husband would not financially help me to buy a house, I decided to scrape the money myself. I had no choice but to sell my valuable jahizieh, which included all the expensive household items I had brought into my marriage.

And at long last, we managed to buy a snug little house.

A few years later, we sold our first house and bought a larger one, which again was made possible only as a result of my relentless perseverance...

Sister, Fataneh - Wedding

"And we made you in pairs...,"

~ H. Quran

"Last night I saw angels beat at the door of the tavern, the clay of Adam, they shaved & with the mold of love they cast...,"

~ Hafez

My younger sister, Fataneh, married a fine man by the name of Houshang, who would in time turn out to be not only a caring husband for Fataneh, but a good friend for all of us in the family, especially me. Their wedding took place under stringent martial law during the Iranian turmoil of 1964 and had to end at midnight.

The 1964 uprising had been instigated by a radical Muslim cleric known as Khomeini, who became an active critic of the Shah's far-reaching series of modernization reforms known as the "White Revolution," which among other things called for land reform, an end to feudalism, extending the right to vote to women, free and compulsory education, the formation of health and literacy corps, and profit-sharing for industrial workers.

Khomeini publicly denounced the government in his fiery sermons, which was a cardinal sin at the time, and he was consequently arrested and imprisoned for 18 months. After his release, due to his continuous recalcitrance, he was eventually sent into exile, which first took him to Turkey, then to Iraq, from whence he continued his revolutionary activities against the modernizing monarch.

The 1964 uprising was to be a dress rehearsal, a storm in the making for the "perfect storm" that was to hit Iran in the guise of the 1979 revolution.

In January of 1978, once again violent demonstrations sprawled, led by religious clerics, who protested an article published by a Tehran newspaper criticizing Khomeini. Institutions viewed as western, such as cinemas and bars were razed to the ground, in one case with over 400 people torched when arsonists set ablaze the Cinema Rex in the southern city of Abadan. Although the revolutionaries were quick to blame the Shah for the atrocity, it is widely believed that they, themselves had been the perpetrators. According to one Middle East expert, Daniel L. Byman, "the movies were thought by the radical Islamists to be an affront to God, encouraging vice and Western-style decadence. So, in August 1978, four Shiite revolutionaries locked the doors of the Cinema Rex in the Iranian city of Abadan and set the theater on fire." It was the single worst terrorist attack to ever occur in history at the time, only to be surpassed by the 1990 Sri Lankan massacre and then the September 11, 2001 terror attacks. It is also widely believed that the event was a key trigger for the Iranian revolution that was to shortly follow.

Deaths during violent protests served to fuel more demonstrations and more deaths in turn, which resulted in an endless, downward-spiraling, vicious cycle.

Khomeini's conservative Shite ideologies began to spread in Iran through smuggled audio cassettes, calling for strikes, boycotts, refusal to pay tax, and even martyrdom, to topple the reformist monarch. Khomeini enthusiasts accused the Shah of destroying Islam and of diluting the indigenous culture through the popularization of Western values, Western clothing, and Western lifestyle.

Separation of sexes in public places, which had thus far been a traditional practice and much prized by the clerics, had been lifted by the monarch, angering the Islamist conservatives. The traditional veil, *hejab*, had been replaced by Western clothes, and women had been encouraged education and a place in the workforce, also anathema to the clerics. Women's deep-seated disenfranchisement had given way to voting rights under the Shah, which was viewed by some as "the last straw that broke the camel's back." An enormously sacrilegious move in the eyes of the Islamist pundits—a cardinal sin.

Due to rampant economic reforms and extensive modernization plans, Iran had ascended to the ranks of a globally formidable industrial economy under the Shah. But ironically, reform in the milieu of participatory political institutions had lagged behind economic progress, creating a vacuum into which the clerics easily slipped, took the lead, and ended the 2,500 years of the Iranian Monarchy.

***

"The world reproduces itself in the course of its eternal gyrations...,"

~ Albert Camus

Fataneh's first child, Pooneh, is very dear to me, and I love her as I love my own daughter, Setareh. Unfortunately, when she was born, probably due to the trauma, she was afflicted with a case of deformity of the ear known as perichondrial hematoma, or "cauliflower ear." She underwent a few surgeries at the Pahlavi Hospital which were not successful. Since her ailment would have been regarded as a handicap in Iran, and therefore she would have been looked upon degradingly, depriving her of advancement in life in Iran, I saw it as my duty to encourage and help them move to America.

Particularly, after Fataneh gave birth to two boys, Arzhang and Hourang, I felt the children would be afforded more opportunity in America. I kept to unceasingly encourage my brother-in-law Houshang to make the move,

"Now that you have these three beautiful children, why don't you consider moving to America, where there is more opportunity for success in life? They deserve better. Think of their future."

Last Chance at Life - Hourang

*"...look within yourself a moment & ask who art
thou? From where doest thou comest...what art
thou...?"*

~ Friedrich Holderlin

When Hourang was born, his older brother Arzhang was stricken with a bad case of black cough caused by an acute case of respiratory infection.

Although a newborn is commonly immune to most illnesses for up to 40 days from birth, Hourang happened to contract the black cough from his brother. The coughing was so severe that the poor baby would turn blue and rendered incapable of keeping his milk, vomiting it out, depriving his body of much-needed nutrition. We were told by his doctors that his prospects of survival were dim at best. Medication did not help, neither did any other medical treatments that we sought.

Family and relatives were terribly worried, desperate, and downcast. The doctors made one final recommendation.

"Your last option for his treatment is to have him fly on a small plane in the hope that the increased oxygen level might help cure him."

Plans were drawn to have the newborn fly on a small plane that daily flew from Shiraz to Bandar Abbas and back, with a stopover in Fasa. We were supposed to have the baby airborne in Shiraz and, after landing in Fasa, we were planning to disembark, and when the plane made the return flight, the baby would be boarded again in Fasa to arrive in Shiraz. The treating doctor saw this as the last hope of survival for the baby.

Then the time for boarding came, and we all went to the airport. But after my sister Fataneh saw the small plane, she was overcome with a sudden panic attack and balked at boarding,

"I'm not flying in that small plane."

We tried to convince her that the plane was safe and flew daily without a hitch, but it was to no avail. After the call to board had been announced, on the spur of the moment, it occurred to me that the only chance of this beautiful and innocent baby's survival was left in my hands. Therefore, I snapped,

"I will take him myself."

With those words, I held the baby tightly in my arms and proceeded to board. Arzhang, who was six years old at the time, insisted,

"Auntie, I'm coming too."

The three of us ended up boarding that small plane and flew to Fasa.

I was glad to have taken Arzhang along. He was good company. I would have been awfully lonely without him.

I was later told that after our small plane had taken off and disappeared in the sky, my daughter, Setareh, had turned to Fataneh threateningly,

"If anything happens to my mother, you won't see the light of day!"

Once we landed, we checked into a nearby quasi-hotel. When the time came to feed the baby, who was hungry and screaming for milk, I realized that due to all the commotion and hysteria, Fataneh had forgotten to give me the sucker that fitted on top of the baby's milk bottle. By then, he was flustered with hunger, and I was at a loss as to what to do. I pleaded to the hotel attendant,

"Can you please help me? I need a sucker to fit this milk bottle, so I can feed the baby."

Luckily, he had an infant of his own and said,

"Don't worry ma'am. I have an extra sucker, in fact, a brand new one. I'll get it for you."

He quickly brought me the sucker and I fed the baby at long last. Miraculously, the baby took his milk without coughing or vomiting. This would have meant that the flight had helped him after all. Arzhang, who was worried sick about his brother, turned to me,

"Auntie, is he better? Will he be fine?"

"Yes, Arzhang, Dearie," said I.

Hours later, we boarded the same plane back to Shiraz.

And Hourang gradually began to recover.

***

"Life is, but a faint imprint on the surface of mystery...,"

~ Annie Dillard

Unlike his brother, Arzhang was incorrigible and unruly, yet smart, and particularly, a gifted speaker as a child. He never hesitated to wreak havoc whenever he came to visit us. He is now a cosmetic surgeon and quite successful at that.

His younger brother, whose life was miraculously spared, was calm and thoughtful as a child. The first words he ever uttered as an infant were the names of my children, Setareh and Arash, because he loved them so much. He left Iran at the age of three and is now living a successful life in America. Today, he is a reputable general surgeon. He is happily married and has three beautiful and smart children.

When you look back in life, you see that the critical moments you live through are the moments you truly live, and they are the moments that you, with love and affection, do something substantial and of consequence.

<u>Loss of a Child</u>

"The Lord gave, & the Lord hath taken away...
blessed be the name of the Lord...,"

~ Job

"The colt dies in harness, taking a new nature in
becoming tame...,"

~ Henry Brooks Adams

Sadra, my first son, was one year old when I bore my second son, Arash, who I believe came to my world for a reason. Having Arash was a blessing in two ways. Firstly, I would eventually lose Sadra due to an enlarged heart condition (cardiomegaly), and having Arash would alleviate some of the pain of losing a son. Secondly, I would never be able to have any more children because of an illness that would strike me later in life, rendering me infertile.

We were devastated when we first learned of Sadra's heart condition. We tried all avenues for a cure with no luck. We tried every doctor we knew and frequented every hospital that could possibly treat him.

Words fail to express the pain and suffering I endured those years when I knew that I would one day soon lose my child. Amidst the agony, though, I had to be strong. I had to put up a sanguine face, pretending that all was fine, so that Sadra would not detect the severity of his illness, the doom that lay in wait for him, and so that he would remain positive.

He turned 7, and the time to start school came. I faced a dilemma. I could not keep him home any longer, because it would raise questions in his mind, turning him suspicious. I was left with no choice but to, with a heavy heart and terrible worry, enroll him in the first grade.

But I first asked the principal to keep him in the office during breaks, so that he would not exert himself playing with his classmates, which would have been detrimental in his condition. Any amount of vigorous physical activity could have ended up in a sudden cardiac arrest. The teachers were gracious, understanding, and accommodating. They heeded my request, kept a vigilant eye on Sadra, and made sure he would refrain from strenuous physical activity.

All this was painful for me beyond imagination. I desperately asked his doctors,

"Will medical treatment, sought abroad in an advanced country, perhaps in England or America, help?

They said, "No."

"There is no chance of cure or survival," they said.

The size of his heart was considerably larger than a normal heart, which left no hope for a medical solution.

Every time I looked at my innocent son, knowing that I would lose him soon, my heart wrenched. My every waking moment was heavy with pain, and I was at a loss as to what to do–an unimaginable loss.

Finally, on a dark gloomy day, and perhaps the saddest day of my life, I saw him collapse. My world came to an end, for I knew too well that that was the end. I picked him up, clutched him in my arms, and ran to the hospital, hysterical. But he had already expired.

I returned home without my beloved son.

The loss of my child was painful in the extreme. Having a 9-year-old and a 6-year-old around made it especially harder to mourn the painful loss of my child. Every time I lost control, sobbing madly, my children hugged me and shrieked with me. I did not want them depressed. I therefore decided to deprive myself of the right to mourn as I wanted to, as I should have, and as I needed to lighten my heart.

I had to come up with some way to vent my pent-up tension, frustration, and pain that would not depress my children. I decided to occupy myself with endless tasks that would leave me no time to think about my loss.

I signed up in a variety of different classes, such as typing and flower making. I even purchased a sewing machine and began to sew unrestrained. For the sake of my children, I had to get back to a normal life. But silently, inside, I continued to burn with an unbridled pain that would not abate.

***

"The whole of life is an act of letting go...,"

~ Buddha

Babylon Revisited

*"May all the Gods whom I settled in their sacred
centers ask daily of Bêl & Nâbu that my days be long
& may they intercede for my welfare. ... The people
of Babylon blessed my kingship, & I settled all the
lands in peaceful abodes...,"*

~ Cyrus The Great

Shahrokh was transferred to Bushehr again. We loaded an army truck with our belongings and left Shiraz for that infamous, sweltering city by the Persian Gulf.

As we were proceeding on the road on a sunny and benign day, we were suddenly overtaken by a deadly sandstorm. A perfectly bright and serene day turned into a dark night in a matter of minutes. In a blink of an eye, sand covered our truck and rendered it immovable. Had the sandstorm lasted any longer, we would have probably been buried alive in that silent and inscrutable dessert.

But the storm came to an abrupt end, and we were miraculously spared.

We had sand all over us: hair, mouth, eyes, and ears. Bathing did not help much either, and we were not able to shed the sand for days.

This time, once in Bushehr, we lived more comfortably than the last. For instance, we were blessed with the convenience of a refrigerator that worked on oil. Having children this time around also helped in living a more normal life as a family.

In the Persian Gulf, we saw majestic British ships anchored offshore. We sailed on boats to reach and see them with curious eyes. They were interesting to see. They had a myriad of unique and interesting merchandise on board to sell which we eagerly purchased.

One day, a few of our friends, Setareh, and I sailed on a boat to a newly arrived British ship. The boat was flat, and not much above water. It was also devoid of any safety rails or guards. As we were sailing along, enjoying the mild breeze with Setareh in my arms, out of nowhere, a sudden storm descended on us, pushing the boat to the left and to the right and causing it to go uncontrollably in circles.

The boat ended up tilting on the side I was sitting on, and I, with Setareh clutched in my arms, lost balance and slipped into the water and began to drown as water covered us. While near-drowning, I felt a hand reach out to me, pulling us out, and saving us. It was the hand of the boat Capitan, who had noticed our fall and had quickly reached out to save us.

That day, seeing the ship and shopping had lost its joy for me. Each glance upon Setareh reminded me of that horrific incident we had just been through. I thanked God over and over again,

"Thank you, Dear Lord, for sparing me and Setareh. Thank you for saving us. Thank you that we are alive."

Needless to say, the thought of that dreadful scene did not cease to haunt me. It deprived me of sleep for days onwards.

Battles with Death

"I never distinguished for a moment between
pleasure & pain...,"

~ Mansour Hallaj

Months passed till one day, I came down with some unknown illness. I had a high fever that would not subside. Doctors in Bushehr were at a loss as to the root cause of my illness. I underwent numerous examinations and tried an array of medications, but my fever would not abate. My doctors finally recommended for me to go to Shiraz to seek further medical treatment. Shahrokh, on account of my mysterious illness and the medical treatment it needed, requested to be transferred to Shiraz, and it was quickly approved. We then moved back to Shiraz where medical treatment was more accessible.

My fever was so debilitating that I could not even sit down. A notable hospital had just been established in Shiraz by the name of Namazi. But people still regarded modern medicine with skepticism and remarked,

"Anyone stepping in that hospital is as good as dead."

I had to convince my family, especially my mother, to consent to my admission to that hospital.

There, I was examined by an Indian doctor named Parasad, who diagnosed me with an acute case of womb infection that required immediate surgery.

I did not dare to disclose the shocking diagnosis with my mother, because I knew she could not bear the news. Therefore, I pretended to be feeling better and asked her to, instead of worrying for me unnecessarily, take a pilgrimage tour of the shrine of the revered Imam Reza in Mashhad, and she eagerly complied.

I underwent a major surgery in my mother's absence, a surgery that was supposed to last only a couple of hours but ended up lasting about 12 hours. I was cut up, the badly infected uterus tissues were detected, and a sample was taken and sent to the lab for examination. Medicine was not as advanced in those days and lab results took much longer than expected.

When the results finally arrived, it was determined that I had contracted a certain bacteria through the mouth, causing genital tuberculosis. It was further revealed that the source of the bacteria had been the cow milk I had drunk in Bushehr. The cow must have been infected, they said. The doctors decided that a hysterectomy, surgical removal of the uterus, should immediately be performed.

I was terribly ill and in much unbearable pain. I remember one day, some of the other patients from other rooms gathered around the propped door that opened to my room and cast pity laden glances on me. They pointed to the many tubes I was intravenously connected to with awe and uttered piteously,

"She won't make it."

I wanted to scream and say,

"No. You're wrong, I will make it. You will see."

But I did not have the breath to utter a single word.

My faith, my love for my children, and the indomitable will to live, kept me alive.

My health gradually improved after the operation. I stayed in the hospital for a month. But I terribly missed my children during my stay. Shahrokh would bring them to the courtyard below my window, and I would walk to the window to get a glimpse of them. I was content with seeing them for a few moments.

I was finally released from the hospital and convalesced for another few months at home. I was worried that my children might have been exposed to the same bacteria. But TBC tests showed that they had not been exposed to the bacteria.

About a year and a half passed, and I started feeling a burning pain in my stomach again. After I underwent thorough medical examinations by Dr. Mohtashami, my second doctor, I was told that I needed immediate surgery again. I underwent another hysterectomy and had an ovary, where eggs are produced, removed, but it was not as difficult as the previous surgery, and I quickly recuperated.

Another two years passed and yet again the pain started haunting me. I was advised by my new physician, my third, Dr. Bolandgharay, to undergo another hysterectomy to remove the second ovary.

This latest surgery would have an enduring negative emotional impact on me. I could not tolerate anyone or any sound. I would experience bouts of depression followed by uncontrollable sobbing. When my mother contacted my doctor, she was told that I should not have any visitors and that I had to stay in quiet surroundings to recover. He also told her that spending time in the countryside and in fresh air would expedite my recovery. I was advised to live a calm life away from tension in the future. Also, for the rest of my life, I have had to use medication to replace the vital functions of my disposed ovaries.

I am forever indebted to my doctors who did not spare any efforts in my treatments. Today, they live in exile in Los Angeles.

I remember one time asking Dr. Mohtashami,

"Doctor, can I still live without PMS?"

He joked,

"I never had any PMS, and I lived!"

It was a funny answer, yet a telling one.

I went through much turmoil and hardship as a young woman but endured them all. Sometimes, I wonder, where did all this resilience emanate from?

Off to Ahvaz

*"There is not any present moment that is
unconnected with some future one. The life of every
man is a continued chain of incidents, each
link...hangs upon the former...often carried on by
secret steps, which our foresight cannot divine...evil
may at some future period bring forth good...good
may bring forth evil, both equally unexpected...,"*

~ *Joseph Addison*

Shahrokh was transferred again, this time to Ahvaz, a city about 500 kilometers northwest of Shiraz.

Ahvaz is the capital of the Khuzestan province. It is inhabited by Persians, Arabs, and Bakhtiaris. Iran's only navigable river, Karun, passes through the middle of the city.

The city has a long history dating back to the Achaemenid period.

During the Umayyad and Abbasid eras, Ahvaz flourished as the home to many well-known scholars at the Academy of Gundishapur, where the modern-day hospital is said to have been first established.

Oil was found near Ahvaz in the early 20th century, and the city grew and prospered as a result of that newfound wealth.

In Ahvaz, we moved to a community of newly built, single-story apartment homes inhabited by army personnel known as *kooye afsaran*. After having gone through so many ordeals, there our lives took a turn for the better. Among the army officer families in the community we lived in, we began to find new friends, whom we started to socialize with. We also happened to find an old friend from Shiraz who was in the poultry business. It is an enigma how people happen to cross paths in life. They lived a good distance away from us, but we still managed to see them regularly.

During winter, we often went to our friends' who had moved there from Shiraz. They always had marinated chicken ready to grill for us. After enjoying grilled chicken, we would go to see the flames that came out of the gas wells, dug in a nearby gas field. I always wondered why that hard-found, invaluable gas was being so senselessly wasted that way, burning, and why could it not be sold to increase the nation's revenues. Over a dozen flames were ablaze simultaneously in a wide plain, emitting such unbearable heat that they were only possible to watch at a distance, and only on winter nights.

Among other favorite excursions we took was sauntering along the Karun River. There was a wide field adjoining the Karun River, where cucumbers were planted. That field drew its nourishment from the fertile silt of the historic river. We savored picking and eating those fresh, crisp cucumbers.

From Shiraz, we often had hordes of friends who came to visit and stay with us. They mostly came during the Nowruz holidays. In a one-story, two-bedroom apartment, accommodation for all of them was a challenge. I remember one time, we had so many guests visiting us that we had to even turn the bath area into a makeshift bedroom!

How enjoyable were those days...? I miss that life that was simple, real, and palpable, even with all the hardships it begot.

As a Civil Servant

"In the depth, I saw ingathered, bound by love in one single volume, that which is dispersed throughout the universe...substances & accidents & their relations...fused together...,"

~Dante

We had a friend who was employed at the Ministry of Health. He happened to be in Ahvaz on a job assignment, and while he was in town, we had him stay with us. Hospitality is a well-known hallmark of the Iranian people and is deeply embedded in Iranian culture. People who know someone in a town they visit seldom go to a hotel; instead, they stay with the friend whom they know.

One day, our visitor made a wild suggestion that surprised me, to say the least,

"You're a smart and perceptive woman. Why haven't you sought employment? Does Shahrokh object to you working?"

I chuckled, "No, he doesn't object to my working a day job. But, what job? And where?"

He returned, smiling,

"I've already found a job for you. There is a vacancy in the laboratory of the Ministry of Health, and I have already taken the liberty of submitting your name with a recommendation."

Elation filled me. I welcomed the opportunity, and I began to work for the first time in my life.

I had no experience, but I did my utmost to quickly learn my assigned duties and to perform to the best of my abilities. My superior, the head of the laboratory, Dr. Arabzadeh, was pleased with my performance, which boosted my self-confidence and further encouraged me to do a good job. I realized that as a woman I, too, could become a productive member of society.

This employment was a building block, a stepping stone, in my mature life. I am forever grateful to my friend's prescience for his help, affording me the opportunity to shape my life for the better.

During the unbearable hot summer months, Ahvaz was almost unlivable. At the end of the school year, the non-natives escaped the heat and left town, seeking refuge in their own hometowns, where the weather was cooler. During the scorching summer months, we too left Ahvaz for Shiraz.

After a few years of living in Ahvaz, duty called for Shahrokh to return to Shiraz again. I also requested a job transfer, which was quickly approved, and I continued my job at the Ministry of Health in Shiraz. There, I had the good fortune of making the acquaintance of a dear colleague, who was also a neighbor. This friendship lasted through the years that I would be living in America but did not end up as I had hoped.

Mother's Sudden Death

"Death eats up all things...young lamb & old sheep...death values a prince no more than a clown... all's fish that comes to the net...,"

~ *Miguel de Cervantes*

"...man lives in time & he is finally devoured by time, for to be born in time is to die...,"

~ *S. H. Nasr*

The pilgrimage season to Karbala, the city in Iraq that hosts the shrine of Imam Hossein, the much-revered grandson of Prophet Mohammad, especially by Shiites, came. People, including relatives and friends of mine, flocked to the Ministry of Health in throngs for the mandatory vaccination required prior to travel to Karbala. Mother had always yearned to, one day, pay homage to the tomb of Imam Hossein. One day I told her of a friend, whom I had seen in the infirmary, preparing to make the much-coveted pilgrimage. This impelled her to think of making the pilgrimage herself. She contacted the friend and asked her about all that the trip entailed.

She excitedly prepared to embark on that long-awaited and much-cherished journey. Arrangements were quickly made. For her safety, we were relieved that she would be traveling with a number of our extended relatives and would not be alone. Finally, she started on a voyage that had been her life-long dream.

After about a month, we received a letter from her, informing us of her return in a week. Her traveling companions arrived next week without Mother. They told us she had decided to stay longer.

All the while, Father had meticulously prepared for Mother's arrival. He

107

had refurbished the house and painted all the rooms. We all waited impatiently for Mother's return, whom we thought would be with us soon.

I was attending an English course at the American Community Center during those days. One afternoon, when the class ended, I saw Shahrokh, who had come after me. I was taken aback and felt it odd for him to come after me, something he had never done before.

"How come you're here?" said I, curiously.

He shrugged his shoulders and did not say much. We stepped into the car and started for home. Shahrokh began to make up a story,

"There has been a bloody uprising in Karbala and some have even been killed. I am worried about your mother's safety. What if she has been among those killed?"

I returned adamantly,

"It's impossible for Mother to be among those killed."

He continued,

"Buildings have been demolished and many have been buried alive under the debris."

I snapped back,

"There is no way for Mother to be among those."

He kept on making up stories, and I kept on refuting them. As we approached Father's house, I noticed a number of cars parked outside by the curb. Worried, I stepped out and ran into the house. I saw a horrid scene of family and friends sobbing relentlessly. My heart dropped and my world turned hazy. I felt like I was in a nightmare from which I could not extricate myself. Everything seemed surreal. I was dazed to the core. The only thing that crossed my mind was,

"How is it possible that while in an innocuous class for only a short time, such a horrendous calamity can descend upon us? Everything was dandy right before I went into my class. How can a joyous life be so upended in the course of just a few short hours? How can misfortune strike so suddenly, so ruthlessly, and so hard? From whence did it come? Why us? Why now? Why? Why...?"

***

"What belongs to the sea, returns to the sea...,"
~ Nereid

During that time, my younger sister, Firoozeh, the youngest member of our family, was preparing hard for the grueling admissions tests required before entering university. The shock of Mother's sudden death came as a devastating blow to her, hampering her passing the entrance examinations.

We were told by those who had arrived and brought the news of Mother's death that Mother had suffered an infection due to unsanitary living conditions in Karbala. The infection had sustained for a few days, and for lack of proper and timely treatment, it had eventually entered her bloodstream, spreading throughout her body, claiming her life in the end. The doctors had apparently failed to detect the cause of her illness, and therefore, had not provided her with the needed medical treatment in time to save her.

Farzad who was occupied with digging artesian wells in the villages surrounding Kerman, after receiving the news of Mother's sudden death, hurried back, hysterical.

As was always the case with a loss in Iran, extensive mourning got underway. People came to soothe us and to sympathize with us with their heartfelt condolences. But nothing could alleviate the heavy pain of Mother's loss. As other pilgrims arrived from Karbala, we desperately rushed to see them, only to hear about how Mother was first struck by the illness, how she spent her last days, how she expired, and how she was laid to rest. We sobbed all we could as we listened, and in the hope of soothing our pain by hearing firsthand accounts of Mother's last days, we asked to be told all there was to know.

As the eldest sister, I felt it incumbent upon me to put on a strong face, to set an example of strength, and to pull my sisters together. For the sake of my younger sisters, I could not continue to mourn and sob endlessly. I had to lead in returning calm and tranquility to our shattered, grief-stricken family.

I, therefore, decided to begin a routine of driving to the quiet surroundings of Gasraldasht Street, where I would park my car, step out, and find a desolate place away from the bystanders. Then I would sob all I could, venting my pain and grief, emptying myself of anger and pity as best I could. I would then return to my family, relieved, calm, and placid-faced.

***

> *"Behold the incredible power of emptying yourself of yourself...,"*
>
> ~ *Sufi Saying*

> *"Life's drama begins with a wail & ends with a sigh...,"*
>
> ~ *Minna Antrim*

Our mourning did not abate until many torturous days later. Losing Mother was difficult in the extreme, and it was made even more difficult because of her passing in a foreign land, all alone, away from us, and with no family member to be with during her last moments.

Not much time passed when one day we were shocked to hear that Father, who had been born and raised in a patriarchal culture, had decided to remarry. Soon after, with the aid of his sisters, he found a woman he liked and was quickly remarried. Having a total stranger replacing Mother was not easy. And it was certainly not helpful in easing the pain of her loss.

With much perseverance, Firoozeh was finally admitted to Jondi Shahpour University in Ahvaz and had to move there. In place of Mother, I would visit her in Ahvaz, to lend her support, and to bolster her mood now that Mother was not around anymore. But no one can replace a mother, no one, not even a sister.

Official Balls

*"All are delectable, sweet sweet sweet, but resign
this land at the end, resign it to its true owner, the
tough one, the seagull, the palaver is finished...,"*

~ T. S. Eliot

Life was spinning unceasingly without a hitch, and events were unfolding as they were meant to.

When living in Shiraz, one of my best, while at the same time worst, memories was the official balls that we attended at the Army Officers Club. The most memorable and exciting of which were the yearly balls that were hosted by the King and the Queen. Those events were titillating beyond description. The King, the Shah of Iran, and his consort, Queen Farah, stood at the front entrance to the ballroom, greeting and shaking hands with the attendees.

Months in advance, I began to look forward to those memorable events, and enthusiastically attended them with Shahrokh. But I would quickly turn downcast when he, as usual, would disappear, leaving me all by myself, with no one to talk to. He, who was exceedingly sociable and a glib talker, would conveniently join and mingle with his own friends, which always left me feeling lonely, forlorn, and dejected. Some would approach me with the same recurring question that I shrank from hearing,

"Are you here alone?"

"No, I'm with my husband," I would answer.

They would continue,

"So, where is he?"

"I have no idea. I think he's busy talking to his friends."

It was at those times that my heart was shattered to pieces. I felt embarrassed when people questioned me about my husband's whereabouts. When approached quizzically, I often looked the other way, shunned them, and chose solitude.

On the way home, I often could not help but burst into tears, which usually resulted in a row that would last for days to come. Simply put, my husband did not have the slightest notion of the importance of courting, or even paying simple attention to his wife and partner in life. He only thought of himself and his own convenience, as if no one and nothing else existed.

While at a party with his friends, he was overly kind and witty. But he was not made to show kindness or love toward his wife. It was as if he were two distinct persons. One, an affable and fun person while with his friends in a social gathering, and two, a cold and rigid person, devoid of any emotions while with his family at home.

I had, by degrees, come to realize that I could not change his ingrained ways due to his old age, and that was how he was molded over his years, and nothing could be done to amend it. With every social gathering approaching, I kept on reminding him,

"Please don't leave me all by myself at this party."

"Yes. Sure. Of course. I won't," he would promise.

But contrary to his word, he would disappear again once at the party. He might have loved and cared for me in his own way, I could not be sure. But since he never showed it with his actions, never expressing amorous emotions, I assumed that he only loved himself and no one else.

New House

"There is no sleep, no pause, but all things renew, germinate & spring...,"

~ R. W. Emerson

We sold our house in the hope of buying a better and larger one. But as always, when facing a momentous decision, we ended up embroiled in endless arguments again. Shahrokh never cared for any change. He was simply content with the way things were. I, on the other hand, craved for and invited change for the better, and sought advancement for myself and my family in life.

I had come to learn to, regardless of how my husband reacted when the time came to make a major decision, take the rein of life in my own hands and steer our lives onto a path that I best saw fit and worthy for our family. But the incessant arguments that were to follow in making each major family decision were taxing, corrosive, and harmful to the collective family psyche. At every turn, instead of encouraging and praising me for striving to improve our lives, he would not hesitate to remain the only dissenting voice, only for the sake of dissenting, which at times proved unbearable.

We were short of money when the time came to buy our new house, our third. My brother, Farzad, stepped up and graciously agreed to help solve our problem with a loan he extended us.

Our new home was a deluxe house, located in a well-known area, in a community of newly built houses called, Tape Television ("Television Hill"). It was a 2-story house, consisting of two independent apartment homes, one on top of the other. We lived in one and rented the other to American expats, who at the time had flooded Iran, working and helping with the extensive ambitious modernization plans of the ruling monarch.

I felt happy and secure in our new home. Setareh was in the 12th grade, busy with her final high school exams. She usually had a friend over to study with, and that gave me peace of mind while I was working. One day, out of the blue, her study companion barged into my office, shaking and panting,

"Setareh has fainted in the shower."

My heart dropped and I turned cold. I did not know how I reached home, and when I did, I found Setareh unconscious, lying down on the floor in the bathroom. With much effort, the two of us raised and dragged her numb body into the street, hoping for a passing car to stop and take us to a hospital.

Terrified and moonstruck, we stood in the street waiting, desperately waving at each passing car, begging them to stop. Shortly after, a car stopped and offered to help. We put her in the car and sped to the Namazi Hospital, where we had family members working as practicing physicians.

Once we arrived at the hospital, we were told that she had been severely dehydrated and had to be injected intravenously to rehydrate. We spent some long hours anxiously waiting for her to recover. It was almost midnight when she gained consciousness and we were finally relieved. We were discharged after 14 painful hours. In hindsight, I now think to myself,

"Where was Shahrokh during all those painful hours?"

After this incident, I noticed that Setareh had turned pale and had lost some weight, too. The day that was to follow happened to be the day that Setareh had to take her final examinations, and despite my dissuading her from attending, she insisted otherwise. Had she not taken the exams, she would have lost a school year, which she would adamantly not accept. Although I was skeptical that she could pass the cumbersome exams, I finally caved in to her wish. But I decided to stand vigilant behind her classroom window, watching her closely to make sure she was well.

She ended up going through the exams victoriously after all!

She, thereafter, entered a one-year preparatory term for collegiate admissions to the Pahlavi University. There, students were mixed, with boys and girls attending classes together. My troubles with Shahrokh started again. He was against Setareh having the remotest relations with boys, not even conversing casually. I was sad that my poor daughter was to be barred from socializing with her classmates.

But I decided to stand by her, and despite Shahrokh's incessant objections, I was willing to allow my daughter some freedom of action as a youngster. I trusted that she was wise enough not to abuse her freedom. But her father continued to be unreasonably suspicious, which led to us arguing all the time again. To solve the dilemma we were faced with, I chose to take a middle course. For instance, when she went to a friend's birthday party, I would consent to her attending, conditionally,

"I'll come to pick you up at eleven o'clock."

I was relieved that she was able to attend the customary social events with her friends while at the same time I kept her under watch. This served to placate Shahrokh and it also served to satisfy Setareh, who at her age, had a right as an adolescent to socialize with her friends.

The oddity of Shahrokh's actions was not new to me anymore. One time before Nowruz, I had baked a variety of delicate pastries, which was a cumbersome and time-consuming task. Then I happened to leave home to visit with some friends. When I returned, I noticed that Shahrokh had mashed all those painfully prepared, delicate pastries in a pot, turning them into some grotesque dough...I just could not believe my eyes. I was simply livid. I only turned and looked at him, speechless. He ruptured with laughter as he often did when caught in a mischievous act,

"Try some. It's delicious!"

A yet simmering feud would be looming, leaving its indelible imprint on my psyche, shaking me to my nerves, leaving me upset for some time. I would sometimes contemplate leaving him, but then I could not. I had two children who needed a father and some semblance of family life, I thought.

Having said much about Shahrokh's shortcomings, now I feel obliged to recount some of his upsides. For instance, I have to admit that he always took the time out to take Setareh and Arash to horse riding classes, martial arts classes, and tennis classes, which I thought was commendable for a father to do. But after Setareh returned from her martial arts class one day with a black eye, I forbade her from attending any more martial arts classes.

I had separately signed up Setareh in a music class to learn to play the violin. Arash, however, turned out to be somewhat unruly and not as corrigible as a teenager. He took a liking in covertly doing the things he liked to do that I had not condoned, such as riding motorcycles with his older friends and frequenting movie theatres in excess and without permission. I was worried about his safety when riding on a motorcycle and never approved it. He often resorted to lying in order to get away with doing the things he most liked to do, and it left me no choice but to resort to punishing him by either cutting his allowance or grounding him, which were not as effective as were meant to be.

Destined for Tehran

*"Henceforth I ask not good-fortune...I myself am
good fortune...henceforth I whimper no more,
postpone no more, need nothing, strong & content, I
travel the open road...,"*

~ Walt Whitman

Time passed as it always did. Setareh passed her collegiate entrance examinations successfully and was admitted to the College of Political Science at Tehran University. I was filled with elation and pride when I first heard the good news. At such times, my world brightened up and I felt I had a reason to live for.

With Setareh's impending move to Tehran, I faced a dilemma. I could not possibly bring myself to send her to Tehran all by herself. Therefore, I decided to request a job transfer to Tehran so that she would not be alone in that large metropolis, and so that she would be living safely with her family while attending university. Shahrokh had recently been retired also, and that left no reason for us to remain behind in Shiraz.

We, consequently, rented out our house in Shiraz and moved to Tehran. I also asked my youngest sister, Firoozeh, who had just graduated from university and could no longer tolerate her stepmother, to join us in moving to Tehran. She happily accepted.

While in Tehran, we changed residences a few times. At first, we rented the second-floor apartment of a two-story building, where the owners resided in the first-floor apartment.

In that building complex, there happened to be a large pool in the middle of the back yard that was partially covered in order to create a lounging area for entertainment during summer evenings, when our landlord's family and friends gathered leisurely, eating, drinking, and passing time through the small hours of the night. We had a long balcony overlooking that pool. I remember one time when Arash was playing with a soccer ball in that balcony, he unintentionally kicked the ball into the middle of their feast, overturning and breaking some glasses and dishes. This accident angered them to the core and created such mayhem that was beyond comprehension.

From that time onward, they turned hostile against us. They kept up with their disparaging remarks, calling us no-good village dwellers, even though they themselves were originally from a town, smaller than Shiraz. Our relationship descended to such lows that they finally asked us to leave.

We moved to another house after that incident. Once we settled in our new home, I resumed work in the personnel department of the central offices of the Ministry of Health. But unlike Shiraz, the work atmosphere was anything but benign. In Shiraz, my colleagues knew me and regarded me with utmost respect, but Tehran was a different story altogether. Sexual harassment was the order of the day. My superiors were shamelessly attempting to make passes at me.

They audaciously showered me with indecent proposals that shook and annoyed me. But I maintained a serious disposition, fending off their proposals, which would eventually keep me out of their good graces, depriving me of career advancement, fringe benefits, overtime, and the like.

Those women who complied with the insidious wishes of their debauched superiors were endowed with endless job perks and benefits. I was appalled and disappointed by the way the governmental offices functioned in Tehran in those days.

Aside from the rampant sexual harassment I suffered at work, I also witnessed an unfair caste system at play, which greatly bothered me. It involved servants and attendants roaming around with utmost servitude, serving tea, beverages, and fetching personal things for the employees, which I thought was abusing. It felt like a microcosm of a feudal system to me. I was depressed and out of place in that immoral environment.

To escape the unsuitable work conditions in the central offices of the Ministry of Health, I requested to be transferred to a smaller office closer to our home in the city of Shemiran, a prominent suburb in the northern part of Tehran, and it was thankfully granted.

I came to enjoy working in the smaller office of the Ministry of Health in the area of Narmak, located on the outskirts of the city. I worked hard and it paid off. I was promoted to the position of office manager. I was happy working alongside doctors, who were genuinely helping those in need.

But working out of yet another office of the Ministry of Health sometime later would prove even more gratifying.

In the new office, my third in Tehran, I had the privilege of working for Dr. Amir Shahi, who headed the laboratory department. He was an exemplary leader with integrity abound, who spared no effort in helping patients. My tenure under him was the most productive and memorable period of my work career at the Ministry of Health. Years later he passed away while residing in exile, in Los Angeles.

Winning a Car

"From his own cup he bade me sup, for such is hospitality...,"

~ Mansour Hallaj

"You're not wrong who deem that my days have been a dream...,"

~ E.A. Poe

The story of the car I won remains an unforgettable part of my career. Mr. Khayami, the iconic founder of Iran National Auto Industry, the first Iranian automaker, had embarked on a marketing campaign, which called for selling a number of Paykan automobiles his factory produced to a limited number of government employees at prices not to exceed the bare cost of manufacturing.

On the appointed day of the much-anticipated lottery, a large number of government employees planned on flocking to the auto factory that was located quite a distance away, out of town, and could only be reached by taking a barely drivable gravel road.

Days in advance, talk of when and how to get there filled our office. Everyone was excited to be there as early as possible to register and win a brand-new car at a reduced price. I only listened quietly, because I had neither any interest nor any intention of attending the promotional event.

But I still went there indifferently around midday, only to observe the excitement, and not much more. A large auditorium was swarming with government employees, edging in, anxious to be selected and called on as winners. I stood to the side and away from the rest of the large crowd.

Mr. Khayami started selecting the lucky winners from the people in the crowd. When he finished, he decided to add one more person to the winners he had just selected. He suddenly pointed to me. I first thought he was pointing to someone behind me. I turned around and looked behind me. There was no one there. When I turned back and caught his eyes, he said into the microphone,

"You. Yes, I'm calling you."

Not having fully grasped what had transpired, I hesitatingly proceeded to approach him on the stage he was standing on. When I reached him, he cast his glance on me,

"Don't you want a car?"

I answered, "Of course, I do."

He asked again, "So why are you hesitant? Let's go."

I was still in a state of shock, but tried to collect myself, and followed the handful of the winners into a bus that drove us to the administrative wing of the factory, where paperwork was processed.

After filling out the application forms, they asked for a deposit. I happened to have my checkbook with me. I thanked God for having had my checkbook with me on that day. I wrote the deposit check and was given instructions as to when and where to come to pay the remaining balance and receive the car.

When I arrived at the office the next day, I saw other employees, who were not selected, chatting. They were sad and disappointed. They had huddled in groups, talking of how they had missed their chances, envying the winners. I yelled,

"I got it. I won."

Apparently, they had missed seeing me at the event. Heads were suddenly turned toward me in sheer disbelief! At first, they thought I was putting them on and did not believe me until I recounted the whole story to them. Looking back at the whole thing, I remember a fitting poem,

There is hope in despair
There is light at the end of the dark, night

When I learned that a school had been opened offering interior design courses, I, having always had a longing for that subject, wasted no time to register and ended up being one of their first graduates. This I did while employed full time and still encumbered by housewife duties.

My younger sister, Firoozeh, was also delighted to find employment with the National Atomic Energy Institute, where she began to work.

European Tours

"There is no new thing under the sun...,"

~ Ecclesiastes

"Nature is a mutable cloud which is always & never the same...,"

~ R. W. Emerson

We traveled to Europe a few times and were able to visit a good many iconic sites there. In Munich, we visited castles that had been built by the order of King Ludwig II of Bavaria, such as Neuschwanstein (New Swan Stone Castle), which he had designed himself at the age of 23. It had been built between 1869 and 1886 on a rugged cliff against a scenic mountain backdrop, intending to "embody the true spirit of the medieval German castle."

It is said that, after visiting Neuschwanstein with his wife while on vacation in Bavaria, Walt Disney was inspired by the 19th-century castle and decided to put his own spin on it for his movies and theme parks.

The saying goes that from 1885 on, foreign banks had threatened the king, who had incurred much debt and defaulted on them, to seize his properties. The king's erratic behavior had led the government of the time to declare him insane, and consequently, he had been deposed. After having been ignominiously deposed, he had committed suicide by drowning himself in Lake Sternberg.

While touring France, we visited all the famous historic sites that we could squeeze into our schedule. We saw the Eiffel Tower, Versailles, Tuileries, Victor Hugo's home, and the Fontainebleau. We spent a day at the Louvre Museum. We sauntered along the famous Champs-Elysees Avenue for hours, frequenting its lovely bustling sidewalk cafes.

We sailed on the Seine River, which flows through the heart of Paris, and saw much of that magical city while cruising on boat, enjoying the refreshing breeze.

Having always been fond of aristocratic lives, I enjoyed visiting old palaces, where people of high birth had once lived in, with my imagination roaming about the kinds of lives they must have lived in those luxurious palaces. In Vienna, we took a tour of the unforgettable palace that the Habsburg dynasty had once lived in.

It was Shahrokh, Firoozeh, and I who first took a tour of Europe. The countries we visited were England, France, and Germany. On subsequent travels, my children accompanied me as well.

One time, when touring Europe with my children, before the famous underwater England-France tunnel was built, we boarded a ship in England that took us and a car we had purchased in Germany to the northern port of Calais in France.

Nowadays, an underwater tunnel connects England to France, considerably shortening the time of travel between the two countries. I hope to one day be able to travel through that tunnel!

We had earlier bought a Ford model car in Germany and taken it to England. On the way back, upon disembarking the ship in France, we drove it to Paris. From there, on our way back to Iran, we drove through Yugoslavia and Turkey.

At the time, Turkey seemed to be a backward country. Drivers were notorious. They did not abide by traffic laws.

One time, when in Istanbul, we took a taxi to go to the central bazaar. The taxi drove us in circles around the spot he had picked us up at and dropped us off at a nearby corner. Once the taxi left, we realized we had been duped and that the central bazaar had been only steps away from where we had earlier stood! Another time, when in Istanbul in a taxi again, I saw the car in front us hit a child and did not even stop. I could not help looking behind in shock to try to see if the child had survived the crash.

On our second trip through Turkey, when driving in our car in the countryside, we saw people hurl stones at cars passing by, asking for cigarettes or money. We had to drive fast to avoid them and could not wait to pass through Turkey. I remember at the time they had gasoline shortages and filling up on gasoline was a challenge.

Turkey today, having cultivated a market economy embracing the international community, is economically a much more advanced country while Iran, having fallen prey to Islamist ideologues of the new regime, secluding herself, has fallen behind.

On my trips to Europe, for my nieces and nephews I avariciously bought fashionable European clothing, especially overcoats and shoes from Galleries Lafayette and Printemps.

My sisters Parvaneh and Fataneh were particularly happy to receive the clothing I brought for their children – they were unique and chic – and you could tell they were European made.

While traveling abroad without my children, Fataneh and her family came to Tehran to keep my children company. They all got along exceedingly well.

That brings me to my recollections of Arash. The only renegade among them was my son, who on occasions indulged in wild forays into uncharted territories. He would venture into driving without a driver's license, for instance, or smoke at school, which was forbidden. To dampen his incorrigible behavior outside, I decided to keep cigarettes and beer at home. Instead of smoking and drinking outside, behind my back, I allowed my children to smoke or drink at home if they ever desired to do so. But thank God, they never abused the freedom I afforded them, and to this day, each has remained a nonsmoker and devoid of a drinking problem.

My son was a sophomore in high school when we moved to Tehran. I noticed that he was indifferent to school and was instead interested in other activities, which greatly worried me. His grades were below average, and as long as he did not concentrate on his studies, his grades would not improve.

After much contemplation, I saw it necessary for him to continue education abroad in a new environment. Iran was beginning to boil with riots at the time, which was also a major distracting factor, making schooling there not appealing. I warned him,

"The only chance you have in life is to first finish high school here and then continue your studies abroad."

To study overseas required passing a grueling examination that needed extensive preparation.

I tried my hardest, as a parent, to raise my children in a way that would lead to a prosperous future, because I strongly believed that as parents, we were duty-bound to help foster a good life for our children. But I was alone in that holy crusade, and for the most part, carried the burden of raising them on my own shoulders, for I had lost hope that Shahrokh would accompany me in fulfilling those essential parental duties.

I kept up encouraging Arash to study hard. I looked forward with anticipation to every exam he took as if I was taking the exam myself. With every exam approaching, I would start having butterflies of my own. I made sure he stayed in his room, preparing for his exams before tending to other leisurely tasks, and he began to comply.

The senior year final exams came to an end. The day the names of those who had passed were to be announced, Arash could not muster the courage to go to school to find out if he had been among them. He must have not had any hopes of passing. To avoid seeing me, he left the house early, unannounced. Then a classmate called excitedly,

"Arash has made it. He has passed!"

I, who had lost hope by then, asked peevishly,

"Are you sure?"

He insisted,

"Yes. Of course. I'm sure."

I still did not believe him and decided to go to his school myself to make sure the good news had been real. His grades had been on the very borderline. He had barely passed, only by a hair's breadth!

Now that high school was behind him, he had to take the examinations required to qualify him to continue his studies abroad. Again, since he was an unruly child, I did not have much hope of him passing the exams. But I had warned him,

"This is your very last chance. If you fail these exams, you'll be stuck in Iran and without much hope of advancement in life."

This time around he truly exerted himself, studied hard, and passed the qualifying exams. This was one of the best things that had ever happened in my life because it drastically changed my son's future for the better.

<u>Migration Begins</u>

"The universe is renewed at every breath, one is annihilated & another takes its place…,"

~ Jami

"There is another sky, ever serene & fair, there is another sunshine, though it be darkness there…,"

~ Emily Dickinson

Fataneh and her husband, Houshang, still lived in Shiraz at the time. When we began entertaining the thoughts of my son's attending school in America, I asked my brother-in-law to, through his relatives who were attending school there, obtain a letter of admission for him. Thereupon, his relatives, living in Houston, Texas, graciously helped obtain for Arash a letter of admission to Sam Houston University.

The all-consuming pattern of sending kids off to the American universities had kicked off before the middle of the 20th century, reaching its height during the early 1970s. Those years mark a time in Iran when most well-to-do families began sending their children to the West for education. It was a time of relative affluence. It was a time of progress and modernization. It was a time when the aggregate economy was making strides toward industrialization. The progressive monarch encouraged modern education for all, male and female alike, which angered the retrograde Islamists. He granted scholarships so that the country's youth could be afforded the best education the West had to offer. It was also a time that all things Western were cherished and in fashion. Most were in love with the West. Some of those who graduated from Western universities returned to help build their country, but a good many chose to stay behind, particularly America.

Meanwhile, I kept encouraging my brother-in-law, who was an employee of the Ministry of Education with not much prospect of advancement, to leave Iran and seek higher education in America. Surprisingly, the rest of the family including my brother, who had himself been educated in Germany, were at odds with me for insisting so. And I could never understand their objections. Perhaps they thought it was difficult to simultaneously attend school and work in a foreign land. I was not sure.

But I did not give up. After constant insisting and arguing on my part, reasoning that attending school in America would result in a better future for my brother-in-law and his family, they finally caved in. They came up with a plan. My brother-in-law decided to first try the new land on his own. And after making the necessary assessments and establishing himself there, the rest of his family would join him. So it was. He set off on this fateful journey alone.

Ironically, since I had been the lone force behind this decision, I began to worry, because if things did not work out as planned, I would have been blamed.

Later, when time came for my sister and her three children to join Houshang in America, I received a disturbing call from him that I had most feared. He called one day, distraught,

"I want to come back. Here, I'm desperately lonely and depressed. I can't take it anymore."

He was adamant. It seemed like he had made up his mind and was determined to come back. I guessed that loneliness had taken its toll on him, and I had to entice him to change his mind. After all, it had been my un-relinquishing insistence that had pushed him over the precipice, into uncharted territory, and I felt it my duty to take action and do something about it. I tried consoling him,

"Are you out of your mind? All new undertakings are difficult at first, but you'll reap the rewards in time. Stay positive. Be patient. Think about the privilege of receiving education in a free and advanced country. Take advantage of your situation. I have no doubt that you and your children will be better off there. Think about their future."

I did my best to dissuade him from returning. I felt that their migration before mine was vital. Had I left before them, there would not have been anyone to encourage and push them to make the move.

When you look back in hindsight, you see certain life-changing moments that have been instrumental in shaping your future. They are the moments when critical decisions are made that change the course of your life for the better or for the worse. They are the moments that set you on a fateful path, from which you may not return.

***

"...knowing how way leads on to way, I doubted if I should ever come back. I shall be telling this with a sigh somewhere ages & ages hence...,"

~ Robert Frost

Fortunately, my brother-in-law stuck it out, decided to stay in America, and asked my sister to join him with their three children.

My sister and her children came to Tehran to set off on their long journey. My nephew, little Hourang, who was only three years old by then, had packed a suitcase full of small cars that he adored. Sadly, it was accidently left behind. When he arrived in America, he was in tears without his toys, my sister called to tell me. I immediately sent them the suitcase, which enlivened him once he received it. I have always loved my sister's children as I love mine. Loving them gives me a feeling of utter satisfaction. Their happiness inebriates me with happiness too.

Once in America, they started living in the student residences in Huntsville, Texas. My brother-in-law, majoring in Mechanical Engineering, attended school at Sam Houston University. With their departure, the road was finally paved for my son to join them next, which he shortly after did.

Arash had promised to study aviation engineering, but once in America, he chose leisurely activities over serious studying and barely graduated from university. He preferred socializing and playing around to studying. Although not thrilled about his doings, I felt I had fulfilled my parental duties to the utmost of my abilities. I had helped him take the first critical steps toward a prosperous future. I had done all I could as a mother; the rest, I thought, should be up to him. I could not control him from halfway around the world, anyway. I had done my part and could do no more. My husband, though, who had not much contributed to Arash's upbringing, only kept complaining about his leaving Iran.

Fortunately, things took a positive turn for my son at long last when he began taking a keen interest in school. He changed majors, and completed university successfully. And I am forever grateful to God for it.

Meanwhile, my daughter, Setareh, together with my youngest sister, Firoozeh, chose to pursue higher education in France. I had arranged for them to be admitted to a boarding school for girls in France.

But they ended up disliking living in France and particularly in the dormitory they were staying at. They complained about the French people neglecting proper hygiene. They said there was only one bath for all the girls in their dormitory, and they had to wait in long lines to use it. It reminded me of a saying I had heard before,

"The reason the French are notorious users of colognes and perfumes, having the best the world can offer, is that they do not bathe as often as they should, so they hide their foul smell under the guise of colognes and perfumes."

For this, among other reasons, they could not get acclimated to living in France, and finally decided to return to Iran shortly after.

I was regularly in touch with my sister and brother-in-law in America to make sure they had adapted to their new environment. I was glad that after having passed the rough initiation period, they began to adjust and settle there. After all, I had been the main instigator and the lone propelling force behind their migration and felt responsible for them. I thanked God that all was going well with them and that they were happy, or else I would have been miserable with a guilty conscience.

I made my first trip to America in the summer of 1977 to visit my sister and her family and also to assess the situation ahead of moving there. I was glad to see their progress. The children were happy, attending school, and Fataneh was busy with her apprenticeship as a hairstylist.

Shortly after I arrived in America, we all went on a road trip, site-seeing through several states. We had not quite reached Mississippi when on August, 16, 1977, the news of Elvis Presley's unexpected death shocked the whole world and dampened our spirits too.

We enjoyed a full day at Houston's famous amusement park known as Six Flags Astro-World, featuring several breathtaking riding prototypes, such as the world's first river rapids ride, and the first suspended-swinging coaster. The children were wary of riding the monstrous roller coaster. Fataneh and Houshang, though, took the ride but turned white and blue after they disembarked, shivering uncontrollably. Having heard that I suffered from chronic back pain, my nephew, Arzhang, tried to dissuade me from taking the roller coaster ride,

"Auntie, please don't do it. It's bad for your back."

I was flattered and proud that he, at his young age, was concerned about my back pain. Finally, our turn came. It was time for my niece, Pooneh, and I, to ride the gigantic roller coaster. The children tried to dissuade us, but we did not heed their pleas and obstinately took the infamous ride.

As always, I was wearing my eyeglasses. Hearts pounding, we slowly reached the cusp of the ride, the ghastly precipice. Then as we began to abruptly descend, due to the sudden jerk, my eyeglasses slipped from my face and flew in the air. I opened my mouth to utter,

"Oh. My eyeglasses"

But before words came out, and after my eyeglasses had come off of my face and were flown in the air, nowhere to be seen, in a matter of a few seconds, they suddenly appeared right before my eyes, and I was able to catch them with a quick snatch!

Although breathtaking and scary, we thoroughly enjoyed that memorable ride.

That joyous trip helped embolden me to make the fateful decision to immigrate to America.

When I returned to Iran, Setareh, who had earlier applied for admission to a university in Louisiana and was accepted, was preparing to leave Iran. She flew to Louisiana, where she started a Master's Program in Media.

With my children gone, I had no inspiration left to remain behind any longer. Shahrokh and I, again, constantly argued regarding our plans for the future. There were times when I felt I needed to divorce him, but could not, partly because divorce carried a negative stigma in our culture, and partly because of my children, whom I did not want to deprive of a father, so I stayed in the marriage. But no one knew how unbearable living with him was.

He was a master of disguise. He showed a good façade. On the surface, he was gregarious, witty, and fun. Almost all who came in contact with him liked him. People thought him the ideal husband and would have thought me insane if they knew I yearned for a divorce. With others, he was an ideal person, but at home he would turn into a drill sergeant: strict, demanding, unreasonably argumentative, and never compliant with any plans I made. His bellicose attitude at home deprived us of peace.

***

"As a man thinks in his heart so is, he...,"

~ Proverbs

Ironically, with all his manly demeanor, he was childishly vulnerable to pain. He would desperately moan whenever he came down with the simplest illness, such as a common case of cold,

"I'm dying. Please help me."

One time, he had a simple case of stomachache. For fear of not surviving, he checked into the army hospital for the night. He would recount later with a grin,

"Do you know what happened last night at the hospital? There was a patient in the bed next to me. The nurse came to administer medication at midnight, asking who Shahrokh was. The guy next to me was fast asleep. I looked at the nurse and pointed to him, so he was given my medication!"

He was bursting with laughter relating his cruel prank while I was shocked and dismayed at his insensitivity toward others.

At times, I thought he must have mistaken our home for a battlefield. There were my children and I on one side, and him confronting us on the other. I could not quite fathom what he was after. Perhaps he wanted a subservient wife, a silent partner with no role in a marriage. Perhaps he wanted to be at the helm with no one contesting him, I could not be sure. It would forever remain an enigma for me.

By and by, the children and I began to get used to his draconian ways. His abrasive discordances started to annoy us less and less. I started making momentous decisions alone and shrugged off his complaints. In retrospect, I am glad that, unlike the wives of earlier generations, I refused to succumb to his whims. But putting up with a constant nag was, nonetheless, a herculean effort.

To the Land of the Free

"Here I'm then, continuing but ever beginning my perennial voyage,"

~ *John Ashbery*

"The Lord goes before you...he will be with you...he will not fail or forsake you,"

~ *Deuteronomy, Torah*

The political situation in Iran began to deteriorate in 1978. A revolution was brewing. There was, everywhere, talk about the Shah leaving the country and Khomeini returning from exile. I could never understand why some people wanted the Shah, a modernizing, European educated, worldly statesman, replaced by a retrograde, medieval, uneducated cleric. Perhaps the hands of the superpowers were at play as they always were in third world countries, and as time would later prove to be the case.

Civil disobedience had become the norm. I had to hurry and proceed with the necessary steps to make the long-anticipated move: immigration to America. I put the house in Shiraz for sale. With the country beginning to boil over, selling a house at the time was no easy task, yet we were in a hurry to sell it. To achieve a quick sale, I had to list it for less than its market price. That house was our only capital, the result of a lifetime of working and saving. But we had no other choice because we were soon making a life-changing move to a foreign land and had to have enough money to survive. We were moving from our homeland where we had grown roots to somewhere we had to start everything anew, not knowing what awaited us.

Our house had many advantages. It was located in a prime location. It was also up to par with Western standards. We had it mostly rented out to American tenants. Luckily, it sold after a few short months.

Selling it served another purpose. It served to burn the bridges behind us, depriving us of a return option. We were then left with only a piece of land in Shiraz that had not increased much in value over the years. I decided to keep it.

During that time, one could feel a grand human change passing over the country. Widespread demonstrations leading to deadly clashes became rampant. It seemed like everyone was scrambling to move abroad, especially to America. It was the hot topic of the day, the subject of common conversation. Poring over the daily papers and journals to learn about migration had become commonplace.

Those who were not able to leave the country read the papers, searching after "For Sale" ads by those who were leaving and had to unload their properties and goods. In the Tehran daily paper, I advertised, "Household Goods for Sale," and was able to quickly sell all of our household goods in no more than a few days. We sold almost all we owned: rugs, furniture, bedroom suites, a sewing machine, and beautiful and irreplaceable chinaware. And people showed up like torrential rain and gobbled up all they saw. The few items that did not sell, with the exception of a few rugs, I gave away to family and friends before I left Iran.

Shahrokh kept up his wrangling and did not cease to be a thorn in my side during those tumultuous days. If anything, his corrosive vacillation further bolstered me to adhere to my plans. He would say,

"Why should we leave Iran for a foreign country, where we can't even speak the language? Why do we have to go where we have no roots in the culture? Why do we have to go where we have no friends?" And many more whys.

Not only was he not any help, his incessant badgering began to take its toll on my nerves, sapping my energies at a time when I needed all my might to make this difficult move. He could not make up his mind one way or the other and had no alternate plans. He could have said, "You go first and I will join later," or, "I will not go, no matter what." But he did not. It seemed he nagged only for the sake of nagging and nothing else.

Only after he realized that he could not thwart my plans, he gave in and conceded to our departure. He booked the flight tickets, Tehran to Newark, New Jersey, on an army cargo plane that regularly hauled military equipment from America to Iran.

> *"Ask & it shall be given you...seek & ye shall*
> *find...knock & it shall be opened unto you...,"*
> *~ Matthew 7:7*

We finally set off to America in 1978, before the revolution flared up. As I was leaving Iran, I had a strong feeling that we would never return. But just in case we did, I had earlier requested my superior in the Ministry of Health to take a one-year leave of absence without salary, which was graciously granted. I had 21 years of commendable service under my belt and was eligible for retirement. But after the revolution, my retirement request would be objected to, and to this very day, despite the untiring efforts of my nephew Fardad, my retirement request has not yet been accepted.

The army cargo plane that we flew on was used to haul large and heavy military equipment such as tanks and artillery. It was oddly expansive, akin to a wide football field with only a few uncomfortable seats. Since there was plenty of space on the plane, I was able to bring along all I could, including our remaining rugs. Shahrokh did not tell me that we were traveling on an army cargo plane until a few days before our departure, or else I could have brought even more of our belongings.

Our nonstop flight to Newark, New Jersey took some 18 torturous hours. From Newark, we boarded yet another plane, a connecting flight to Houston, and from there, we drove to our final destination, Huntsville, Texas, almost half-way around the globe from where we began. Our bodies were numb from fatigue. Our minds were in a surreal daze.

First Venture - Motel

"Two roads diverged in a wood & I took the one less traveled by & that has made all the difference…,"

~ Robert Frost

Once you leave your country, culture, job, friends, and tear all the ties that have fastened you a lifetime, you need to stay strong with a steel-like resolve to overcome new challenges and continue your life. Your education, work experience, laws, norms, and moral standards will most likely not be embraced in the new country. Therefore, you need to start all over. You are first given a nine-digit number, your social security, your new identity.

It becomes incumbent upon you to assimilate in all aspects, not the other way around, because it is you who has taken refuge in a new land. You become like a newborn who has to start from zero, walking and talking. But a newborn who has decided to be a newborn again on his own accord. The difference is, a newborn has no recollection of a past to break loose from, but you do, and that is much more difficult to overcome.

In the new land, a host of new basic issues needs to be addressed, such as,

"Which city or district to live in? Where to rent an apartment? Where to shop for food provisions? What food items to buy? Where to learn the new language? Where to shop for other living items, economically? How to commute? Where to buy a car? How do you get your driver's license? Where do you bank?"

And then you have to learn the laws so you remain a law-abiding citizen – which is a whole new realm in and of itself.

What exacerbated our difficult adjustment to our new surroundings as a family was having a husband who not only refused to understand the needed assimilation, rejecting to shoulder his share of the difficulties, but made it hard for me and my children to do so. I understood the hardships and dealt with them the best I could, but my husband did not and would not.

He expected to, as in the old country, live the privileged life of a senior army officer. My problems became twofold now: one, struggling with my personal immigration and assimilation challenges, and two, dealing with my husband's corrosive attitude which outweighed the first.

He would start a row on a thing as immaterial as greeting our language teacher and bidding him farewell, saying, "See you tomorrow." He would complain, "Why did you tell him, see you tomorrow?" It became an obsession for him to downplay anything and everything that this land had to offer. It also angered him that we, the immigrants, had to assimilate. For instance, seeing other compatriots working menial jobs would drive him livid mad.

To be able to stay in America legally beyond the expiration date of our tourist visas, we were referred to an attorney to apply for Permanent Residency. We were told that to obtain Permanent Residency, we had to apply for Immigrant Investor Visas, which meant investing in some business in America.

The political turmoil in Iran had worsened in a downward vicious spiral. Anti-American rhetoric and overtures had become part and parcel of the propaganda, spinning daily by the new regime, fanning the fire of resentment toward Iranians in America. The pervading dislike of Iranians had made it difficult for us in America to live and work. At the time, we were simply not in favor in America. But we were determined to stay here, no matter what the consequences.

To make the matters worse, the amount of investment required for the Immigrant Investor Visas had more than doubled at the time. This meant that, with our limited financial resources, we had to partner up with someone to be able to afford investing in a decent, sizable business. We therefore decided to start a business with my brother-in-law Houshang, who had just graduated from university. He had a fair command of English and was reasonably familiar with the ways in America. Starting a business in a land that did not seem friendly undoubtedly posed great risks, but we had no other choice.

***

"Who doth not work shall not eat...,"

~ R. W. Emerson

Since we, the Iranian expats, had lost our grace, we were generally being looked down on, even by attorneys. Consequently, retaining an unbiased attorney had become yet another challenging task.

We kept on searching for a business to purchase. Finally, an opportunity arose, and we set our sights on buying a motel located next to a busy highway that connected Huntsville to Houston. My husband began to complain again,

"Why do we have to live in this foreign land? Why did we have to leave our home country? Why do we have to invest in a business we know nothing about? Why?" And why? And why?

He also resented that I always accompanied my brother-in-law in searching for a business and participated in the meetings that it would beget. He could not understand that I had no choice in the matter. Houshang, who was the only one who could speak English, had to lead the search, and as his partner, I had to be by his side.

After conducting the necessary due diligence, we finally purchased the motel that we had earlier eyed and began to work.

We started living in a two-story building behind the motel's office that had a living room and a kitchen on the first floor and two bedrooms on the second floor. This marked the beginning of a drastically new way of life for us. We had to do things we never before dreamt of. For instance, we daily had to clean the guest rooms and bathrooms and change the linen and wash them. After the cleaning was done, I often sat in the office, waiting for guests to arrive.

With the advent of the motel venture, Shahrokh's behavior got from bad to worse. He would have rather died than to see us cleaning rooms and bathrooms, or changing bedsheets. He thought such work was only befitting a servant and way beneath us. But we could not afford to hire extra help, and had we done so, we would not have been able to draw any income to live on.

Houshang and I decided to divide the daily management tasks. On the days I cleaned the rooms, changed and washed the bed sheets, he would stay in the office receiving customers during the night and vice versa.

In a drastic turn of events, my husband, previously a decorated army officer, and I, a long-time civil servant, had become motel owners in that nick of the woods, on a freeway that stretched from Huntsville to Houston, on the other side of the globe, thousands of miles away from where we had lived before.

I reasonably succeeded in adjusting to the tough currents that our new lives had imposed on us, but Shahrokh never could. His resentment increased by the day and one day, as a sign of protest, he decided to return to Iran. He could not bring himself to understand that, once again, we had to start our lives from zero.

In the process of adjusting to the new surroundings, other auxiliary issues would arise from time to time that we had to deal with.

They are some of the same issues that most immigrant parents have had to grapple with, namely, raising children in America. Coming from predominantly traditional environments, immigrant parents have usually found the freedom afforded youngsters in America as excessive. The laxed ways the young dress and conduct themselves have often been hard to swallow by them.

On the other hand, the immigrant children, especially teenagers, in conforming to the new environment, have often felt compelled to emulate their peers, resulting in discordances with their parents.

I often supported my niece Pooneh as a teenager while at the same time tried to lessen any tensions emanating from adjusting to a new culture. As she grew older, she decided to strike a life of her own, independent of her family. While supporting her in whatever way I could, I continued to keep a vigilant eye on her. And I continued to be proud of her accomplishments in life.

After my husband's acrimonious departure, I began to worry that I might be seen in a negative light by our relatives in Iran. I often wondered how I would be judged back home, by both friend and foe. I believe it has to do with our culture that we, Iranians, excessively worry about how we are thought of and judged by others, and I guess I was no exception.

After some time, the need to commute arose. Back in Iran, one could manage without a car, but here it was almost impossible. I could not do without a car. I searched and finally found a car I liked. But I thought I had to pay the full price in cash as was the norm in Iran. Therefore, I purchased a brand-new Ford Ltd, a six-cylinder car with full options, for $8,000 in cash. I thoroughly enjoyed driving it for the next 8 years. Later, I would come to learn that in America, cars are generally purchased on credit! And I would also come to realize that in fact most things are usually bought on credit in this country, so that one can build a good credit record.

I have great memories with that car. I took two long enjoyable trips across many states with that car, one of which was a family road trip through several states, all the way to Oregon, where we visited the famous Newberry Volcano.

Second Venture - Grocery Market

"While man's desires & aspirations stir...he cannot choose but err...,"

~ Goethe

During those turbulent times, my past neighbor and old friend from the Ministry of Health, together with her husband and children, moved to California. We were the best of friends in Shiraz, and perhaps more like family than friends, constantly socializing and spending jolly times together.

In order to obtain the much-coveted status of Permanent Residency, they were also looking to find a business to invest in. Since they were short of capital, they asked if I would be interested to join them as a partner. I welcomed the opportunity eagerly. I had known them for many years and had trust in their honesty and integrity. I felt certain they would treat me fairly.

Thereupon, I assigned the motel to my sister and her husband and got ready to join my friends in California. It was agreed that, in my absence, Houshang would be paid additionally for his extra time and effort that he needed to spend to run the motel. This would leave almost no income for me to receive from the motel business. But I felt I had no other choice.

You might ask, why did I feel compelled to make that move? I would have to say that the underlying reason for my move had my husband's imprint on it.

I had always been known for my integrity and high morals among family and friends. With my husband gone back in anger, I suspected he might entertain vile thoughts and ruin my good name if I stayed behind in Huntsville. He had left protesting the close working relationship I had developed with my brother-in-law. Therefore, the main reason for accepting my friends' offer and to move to California was to keep my reputation intact and to not give fodder to my husband, whose darker side was ever ready to spin baseless gossip, tarnishing me. Therefore, I readily accepted my friends' offer of partnership in California.

I rented a U-Haul trailer, filled it with household goods, towed it behind my car, left Huntsville, and headed west, toward the sunset. Upon arrival in California, I rented an apartment and quickly got settled.

My friends had already found a grocery market to purchase. And little did they know what a cumbersome task running a grocery store would be.

Hardly able to speak the language, we showed up at an attorney's office to sign the purchase agreement. By signing the long legal documents that we could not read and barely understood, we unknowingly pledged to only hire employees from the local labor union. This would forbid us in the future to employ anyone other than those approved by the labor union, which would, in the months to come, result in labor issues, including exorbitant labor costs. This pledge was deliberately not explained to us by the selling agent for fear that it could be a deal breaker. That goes to show the extent to which not fully knowing the native language can harm you, and how some can take advantage of that shortcoming.

We purchased the grocery market and began the daily running of a business which would prove to be far from easy. During the first few months of the operation, we worked with enthusiasm, arranging products on the shelves, cleaning, scrubbing, and cleaning again. We were happy and thought we had bought a good business.

But when confronted by the heavy workload, the bubble was busted. My partner began dodging work. Instead, he resorted to his son to work in his place. I, on the other hand, had no one to share the burden of the strenuous workload with, and as an equal partner, I was expected to match the work of my partner and his son, combined.

Keeping up with the names of the myriad of grocery items we had to purchase, place on shelves, and sell, in itself was a challenge. After some 40 years of living in America, I am still not wholly familiar with all the products a grocery store offers! I recall one day a customer, asking me,

"Excuse me, where can I find the horseradish?"

Not being able to understand what the customer was asking for, I questioned if the item was edible. He laughed and said, yes, and that it was a kind of sauce. I turned to my partner's son in desperation, hoping that he, who was younger and more familiar with the English language, might know,

"Can you please answer the customer?"

He pondered for a few long seconds and then turned to the customer,

"I do know that the radishes are in the fresh vegetable aisle. But I have no idea where the horse could be!"

The customer, who saw our sincerity in not being wholly familiar with the grocery business, said with a kind grin,

"No problem. Let's go find them together."

He quickly found the horseradish.

"Here they are. These are called horseradish."

We all laughed and thanked him profusely,

"Oh. Thank you so much. Thank you so much."

That turned out to be a comical incident, one to be always remembered! Incidents like those were further proof that Americans are generally kind-hearted and sincere.

It was also during this time that I happened to be witness to an earthquake. I was in my apartment when it struck. It was so powerful that it threw me to the left and to the right, hitting the walls in the hallway.

The grocery market was not immune to the earthquake either. Shelves were overturned, merchandise was damaged, and much cleaning had to be done. But luckily no injuries were suffered by anyone.

As I was struggling with the cumbersome challenges this new venture imposed on me, my partner and my lifelong friend, in a turnabout face, began to change from the kind, loving person I knew, to a belligerent enemy for no particular rhyme or reason that I could discern.

It reminds me of a saying that,

"If you truly want to get to know someone, either travel with them or do business with them."

Ironically, back in Iran, we had joyfully travelled many a time together in the past, and I had at no time been witness to anything but kindness and amity from him and his family.

Those who have started a business can appreciate how difficult a task it may be in the beginning. To succeed, impediments need to be overcome with patience, perseverance, and cooperation. New ideas have to be explored from time to time to improve the business. Hence, a spirit of teamwork and understanding is needed to succeed.

For instance, to boost sales, I suggested turning the area in the front of the grocery store to a café, serving coffee and pastries, but he would not consent.

My partner's main point of contention was that since he and his son were both working in the grocery store, I had to match them in working. I was left with no choice but to ask my daughter, Setareh, to come to my aide.

She graciously agreed, quit school, and moved from Louisiana to California, only to bail me out. After all, this venture was a family asset, I thought, which my children had a stake in, too. Nevertheless, my daughter had always been my guardian angel and selfless protector. Her presence by my side was a God-sent gift. She alleviated some of my burden. Since she was easy to get along with, it was agreed that my partner would deal with her instead of me. Her presence also afforded me the opportunity to take a few hours off to see a doctor.

I can remember many incidents of abuse I endured while in partnership with this lifelong so-called friend. He expected me to lift and move heavy boxes of melons, for instance. A female should not be expected to perform such unfit, heavy tasks. I turned to his wife, who was my dearest friend at one time, asking her to talk to her husband and persuade him to refrain from putting so much pressure on me, but she balked at mitigating the tense work conditions, reasoning,

"You two have to work it out yourselves. I don't want to interfere in your partnership."

I turned to his older son who had lived longer in America and seemed to be more reasonable,

"Can you please talk to your father and ask him to amend his ways?"

He would shake his head,

"My father won't listen to anyone. I'm sorry. There is nothing I can do."

The tension at work was further exacerbated by the hostage crisis in Iran. Iranians were singled out and harassed. Stones were hurled into our windows as if we were responsible for the new Iranian government's malignant conduct vis-a-vis the American diplomats in Iran, who were unjustly kept in captivity for 444 days.

The tension finally took its toll on me. I had pain in my back and legs. My sciatic nerve started to hurt. When family and friends called to see how I was making out, I could not but break down crying.

My nerves were giving in under the unbearable weight of stress. I was emotionally in shambles. My health was affected. I lost much weight and felt unwell.

***

"Never to suffer would never to have been blessed...,"

~ E. A. Poe

On a lighter note, as I recount my horrible ordeal during those horrible days, I remember a comical incident that happened at that time. I was advised by family and friends that whenever anyone asked where I was from, it would be best to refrain from saying, "Iran." I dislike lying as a general rule. But one day, I impulsively heeded their advice when shopping in a boutique. While standing at the check-out counter, paying for the merchandise I had bought, the clerk approached me, curiously,

"Where're you from?"

"Greece," I snapped without even thinking.

Excited, she left her post for the backroom,

"Oh great. We have a Greek employee here. I will bring her in a second, so you two can get acquainted."

Blood rushed into my face, and I turned crimson. As the clerk was jovially walking to fetch her Greek co-worker to meet me, I quickly ran out of the store, stepped into my car, and sped away. I never again pretended to be anything but Iranian. I was ashamed of myself and regretted that I had lied.

At times, I was faced with folks who seemed stirred, seeing a foreigner. They would inquire in a disparaging tone,

"Where are you from?"

I would abruptly return,

"I am American. You came before me, and I came after you! That's all!"

This would invariably put them in their place!

Back to the grocery market venture. The exorbitant labor cost that we had to incur, due to labor union obligations we had unknowingly consented to, began to drain our income, adding to our frustrations. We were hard at work with hardly any income to show for. I suggested retaining an attorney to legally relieve ourselves from the yoke of the labor union, but my partner would not hear any of it. Again, I brought up the idea of opening an outdoor café, but he said no again. He was averse to anything that I suggested.

As the corrosive situation at work worsened, I could no longer handle the workload that my partner had ruthlessly imposed on me, nor could I bear being bullied by him. I was ready to just walk out. One day, I asked him to buy my share of the business. He retorted sarcastically,

"No. Are you trying to escape?"

I said, "Well, then let me buy your share."

He returned, laconically, "No. Are you trying to run me out?"

It seemed like a no-win situation.

I knew our contract had stipulated that in case one of the partners was desirous to sell his share, the other partner had the "first-right-of-refusal," meaning that he had the first option to buy out the selling partner, and in case he failed to exercise that right, the selling partner could sell to a third party outside of the partnership.

I had no choice but to threaten him,

"Look. I want to sell my share to save my life from this nightmarish partnership and your wicked ways. I cannot continue working with you. If you don't buy my share, I know that as stipulated in our agreement, I'm entitled to sell my share to a stranger."

Only then did he, wary of having a total stranger as his partner, agree to sell the business together with me to someone outside of our partnership. Unfortunately, by his acrimonious actions that soured our working relationship, he ruined the chances of success for the two of us in a business that had reasonable prospects, had we stuck it out and worked amiably.

After I sold my share, because of the bitter ordeal I had gone through, I returned to Huntsville, unwell and in low spirits.

We severed our relations for a long time. Years later, my partner's wife surprised me with a call,

"I'm devastated. My husband has been diagnosed with a terminal case of abdominal cancer and doesn't have much chance of survival. Before he dies, I would like to ask you, as an old friend, to please forgive him for having mistreated you during those years. Will you please?"

He must be too proud to call himself, I thought.

I also thought to myself,

"Where were you when he was torturing me?"

I simply said,

"Who am I to forgive? It's God who forgives."

***

> *"My love to God leaves me no time to hate the devil...,"*
>
> ~ *Rābi'a of Basra*

Back to Huntsville

*"The sun also ariseth & the sun goeth down &
hasteth to the place it arose...,"*

~ Ecclesiastes

My youngest sister, Firoozeh, had also left Iran to join me in California, where she started training as a hairstylist, which she greatly enjoyed. After I quit the grocery business in California, she, having completed her training as a licensed hairstylist, accompanied me in returning to Huntsville, Texas.

We had no sooner arrived in Huntsville than my brother-in-law Houshang, exhausted from managing the motel, asked to take some time off. He promptly handed me the keys to the motel and said,

"Glad to have you back. It's your turn, now."

After breaking loose from a dreadful partnership, exhausted and in shambles both physically and mentally, I accepted the responsibility of running the motel again. The work, although hard, felt more bearable this time around, I guess because no one was breathing down my neck, getting on my nerves, like in California. I resumed the mundane work alone, which involved the daily cleaning routine and waiting for the new arrivals of mostly uncouth truck drivers until midnight. Seeing some of those rough-looking truckers gave me chills. I was scared and worried for my safety. For my safety, I decided to have the television turned on high volume in the room behind the reception area. And pretending that I was not alone, I would sometimes even yell,

"I'm coming. Just a minute."

About the time of my departure from California, the diplomatic relations between Iran and America had sunk to an all-time low. My daughter

Setareh was distraught by the hostile anti-Iranian mood that had permeated America at the time. She, therefore, decided to part ways with us and move to Australia, and no matter how much I tried, I was not able to dissuade her from changing her mind. She had a close friend that she planned to join in Australia. Her departure was hard on me, and I had to cope with her absence with a heavy heart, which was not easy. But I had no choice except to abide by what destiny had in store for me.

***

"Life is a long rehearsal for a play that'll never come...,"

~ From 'Amélie'

My Husband Returns

"If you're not already dead, forgive. Rancor is heavy, leave it on earth... die light,"

~ J. P. Sartre

"Amend your ways & your doings...,"

~ Jeremiah

During my stay in California, and subsequently in Huntsville, I received numerous letters from my husband who had gone back to Iran. Back then, the primary mode of communication was the letter. His letters were akin to love letters, expressing endless apologies for having left me, asking me to forgive him for his vile behavior during our married years,

"I'm sorry for the way I've treated you. I truly regret having mistreated you. I want to come back and make it up to you. Please do forgive me."

As I usually confide in my children, I shared one of the letters with Setareh who was in Europe at the time, about to travel to Australia, asking for her thoughts. Her reaction was,

"Father will never change. He may be a slick writer, but the minute he comes back, he'll revert to his old ways."

But I was fooled again. I thought that perhaps his being away from his family might have taught him a lesson, so I felt obliged to give him another chance.

I began to make the overarching arrangements for his return. He first left Iran for France, where he stayed with a friend while he waited for my help in securing a visa for his return. Iranians were generally denied visas without exception at the American consulates. Therefore, I had to engage a powerful and costly attorney to help obtain a visa to Mexico for him first, which took several months. From there, the same attorney made arrangements for his return to the United States.

After he returned to America, not much time passed before I realized that my daughter had been right all along. Not only had he not improved an iota, he had turned for the worse. Unbearable complaints, naggings, and arguments resumed once again,

"Why do you have to clean the guest rooms? Why do you have to sit behind the reception desk all alone till midnight?" And many more whys.

Not only did his return not bring me any peace, but it further exacerbated my troubles. He had completely forgotten all about the letters he had written, begging for forgiveness, promising to amend his ways.

While still in the motel business, one day it occurred to me that it might not be a bad idea to build a gas station on the lot adjacent to the motel. Having been located on a major freeway, it could have easily drawn customers from the pool of motorists driving by. The traffic generated by the gas station would have also boosted the motel business. A synergy could have developed between the two businesses. My partner Houshang did not like the idea, though, and I did not think it wise to invest in a property that we together owned. I did not want to jeopardize our amiable family relations in any way.

Not much longer, we both decided to sell the motel and move to Houston.

We rented a second-floor apartment in Houston. My youngest sister Firoozeh who was still living with us, found a suitable job there, and I also started working in a large department store by the name of Pala Royal. I was hired as a salesperson in the jewelry department. I worked hard and achieved record sales. One time, after reviewing my performance, the manager heading my department approached me with a sarcastic grin,

"Did you know something? You make more money than I do."

Soon after, he hired two more salespersons in my department, which considerably diluted my income!

One of the peculiarities of working at Pala Royal for me was the weekly, early morning meetings of all the salespersons. In those meetings, shopliftings and employee thefts caught on camera were shown. It was shown how an employee would surreptitiously insert a hundred-dollar bill into her sleeve. Minutes later, she would be in the office, seeing her mischief on camera, and next, the arrival of police, the handcuffing, and the shameful parading before her peers would ensue, leaving us agape. I found those meetings bizarre because the thought of anyone stealing had never crossed my mind. It was not in my make-up to even think of such disgraceful conduct. How can a decent human being steal? But gradually I came to the sad realization that not all people were righteous, and some stole with no regrets.

To tell a funny story, one day, a customer asked me,

"Where can I find the jackets?"

I innocently pointed to the clothing department and said,

"That's where the jackets are."

She laughed,

"Oh no. A jacket is a piece of jewelry that wraps around other jewelry!"

Embarrassed, I then learned what a jewelry jacket was and that it was different from a jacket, one wore.

Sister, Firoozeh - Wedding

"…that is happiness…to be dissolved into something complete & great…,"

~ From 'My Ántonia'

Firoozeh made the acquaintance of a young Iranian man through a friend of hers back home. Their friendship started when I was occupied with managing the motel, and it finally ended up in their marriage in Houston.

I arranged a small, yet quite memorable wedding ceremony for them. My other sister, Fataneh, made her wedding gown, and I managed the wedding ceremonies and invited family and friends. My cousins from California and Louisiana were among the attendees. Sadly, my daughter Setareh was in Australia at the time and her absence was discernible.

For the wedding ceremony and the dinner reception that followed, I rented the clubhouse of the apartment complex we lived in. I arranged the traditional Iranian wedding ceremony spread known as *sofreh aghd*, which turned out to be remarkable by all accounts. An officiant was present to perform the Islamic ceremony and document the wedding.

Firoozeh, who had lived with us most of her adult life after college, finally left us and started her married life with her husband, Hamid. I was happy that she had finally formed a family of her own. She had always been like a daughter to me. After we lost Mother, I always had her near me and under my auspices. Her absence from my life was now sadly palpable.

The Fire Fiasco

"Life is not so much about beginnings & endings as it's about going on & on & on...,"

~ A. Quindlen

One day, as I was sitting on the balcony of our Houston apartment overlooking a park, deep in thought, I noticed a bystander approaching me and screaming frantically,

"Fire! Fire!"

I did not know the meaning of the word "fire" because I never before had to use that word, so I indifferently and calmly stayed still. He yelled louder, pointing to the neighbor's apartment,

"There is a fire, hurry, get out!"

When I turned around to see our neighbor's apartment, I saw flames coming out of the windows. I was jarred with fright,

"Shahrokh... Shahrokh... the next door apartment is on fire... we have to get out, hurry,"

Americans, usually without expecting anything in return, do truly come to one's aid in time of need. As good Samaritans, they consider it their civic duty to help those in need, as if it is part and parcel of their culture to help others. I have always admired this noble American trait. In a matter of seconds, neighbors and onlookers pitched in and hauled our belongings to a safe place in the parking lot. Afterwards, my husband and I discussed paying them,

"Well, they worked so hard, moving our heavy furniture and the rest of our stuff. Should we pay them?" he asked.

"I've no idea," I returned.

But it turned out that their act had been purely humanitarian and not for money.

***

"In nature, there is prayer in every action...,"

~ R. W. Emerson

Fire engines soon arrived and the fire was successfully extinguished. But the neighbor's apartment had been badly scorched. Smoke and black dust were everywhere, haunting us for some time to come. It took days before life was back-to-normal again.

Other things that come to my mind during this period are buying our first house in America, and my daughter's return from Australia. After having lived in a rental apartment for years, we decided to buy a house in a suburb of Houston. We found a three-bedroom, one-story house in a pristine cul-de-sac located in a suburb of Houston that we liked. We purchased the house and moved there. My sister Fataneh and her husband also bought a house in that subdivision, and we lived there as neighbors.

Setareh, who by this time had been worn out under the weight of loneliness in Australia, decided to return to America. She would later retort,

"Loneliness is not tolerable, not even in paradise."

Lastly, my thoughts go back to my dear niece, who has always been very dear to me. As mentioned before, from a young age Pooneh had chosen an independent life separate from her parents. I understood her and tried to be of help to her and impart her my best advice.

I remember Pooneh working hard and saving money to buy a red convertible Ford Mustang, which was the sports car of choice back then. The kind-hearted person that she was and still is, she used to have the family members take turns (since they all could not get in the car together) in riding up and down the famous Westheimer Road of Houston in her new car, so they could share in the joy of riding in that beautiful automobile.

She has been a maverick since childhood. In addition to me, she had, at an early age, been another driving force behind her parents' immigration to America. I took notice of her progress with a keen eye and continued to bask in her achievements in life.

When she came of age, she was attracted to a young, handsome Iranian man with blue eyes, a much-relished feature in a man by Iranian women, and they were quickly married.

Again, I took immense pleasure in arranging a beautiful traditional wedding spread for her, who was living with her parents in the same subdivision we lived in. I further arranged for her wedding cake but left it up to her to select the details. It turned out to be one of a kind. It was a multi-tiered cake with a running-water fountain in the middle.

The groom was never quite approved by the collective family due to the nature of the business he was in. He owned a nude bar which was terribly at odds with our culture and moral standards. He had promised to change professions once married, but did not follow through with his promise after marriage. This quickly soured their marital relations. Unfortunately, their marriage did not last long, and they divorced in less than a year.

<u>A Separation</u>

"Non, rien de rien...Non, je ne regrette rien...Je repars à zero...,"

~ *Edith Piaf*

"Why should the setting be injurious to the sun & the moon...?"

~ *Rumi*

I was working extra hard those days, trying to prove myself in the new environment. But as a new immigrant, lacking a decent command of English and not being wholly familiar with life in a new culture, it was all the more difficult. I often had to work harder than my American peers just to be accepted. It was taxing. But what aggravated it further was having to put up with my husband's hairsplitting antics when I would return home after a tough day's work.

He had recently purchased a car and had gotten in a habit of, without telling us where he was headed, roaming around the city at will, seemingly just to intimidate us. One time, he left the house and did not return till nightfall. We waited, worried and at a loss, not knowing what to do. First, my children called our relatives in Houston, but he was not there. After much brainstorming, we guessed that he might have gone to visit a relative in Louisiana. My children called our relative down in Louisiana. After pleasantries, they said,

"We're worried sick. Shahrokh left the house this morning and hasn't returned. Is he there by any chance?"

Our friend, who was moved by hearing my children's pleading voices, said with a chuckle,

"Yes, he is here, to tell you the truth. But he has asked me not to tell you he is here."

We were relieved. And he returned after a few days.

He continued his surprise excursions from time to time until one day he worried us again by leaving the house,

"I'm going out of town for a few days."

"Where to?" I asked desperately.

"Well, somewhere," he returned, sarcastically.

"How long will you be gone for?" insisted I.

"Don't know."

This time, he drove to Kansas to visit a woman relative of mine and her husband, who happened to have marital problems. He had decided to mediate between the husband and the wife. To help them overcome their differences and mend fences, he had felt he needed to spend time with them. Therefore, he conveniently brought them back with him without even asking me,

"You two get your stuff ready. We're going to Houston and you'll stay with me until you work things out."

He, audaciously, took it upon himself to bring that family of three to my house to stay until they resolved their marital issues, without any consideration for how my children or I felt about having three indefinite house visitors.

"Shahrokh, how could you invite them without letting me know first?" I complained.

"Well, it was the right thing to do."

My husband wore the facade of a nice, jovial fellow, under which people knew not what laid.

The uninvited house guests, including their five-month-old baby, who would not stop crying, stayed with us for months. Having them in our one-story bungalow house while my children and I had to wake up early to go to work was terribly inconvenient to say the least.

What made it even worse was when the husband, an alcoholic and a rowdy foul-mouth, was inebriated at night and would not hesitate to blurt expletives at his wife and her family, who happened to be my relatives too. His obnoxious behavior at times led to heated rows between him and my husband too, which created a fiasco that further deprived me and my children of badly needed peace and quiet.

One night, when our house guest was drunk, throwing obscenities at will with no restraints, I felt I'd had it. I could not control myself any longer and snapped,

"I've had it with you. You cannot stay here any longer. Get the hell out. Now."

After realizing that I truly meant what I said, he collected his belongings and grudgingly left the house. We were all relieved at his departure, and peace was once again restored at long last. But a few hours later, the phone rang. I picked up the phone and heard a stranger saying,

"Hello...there is a vehicle here with license plate number...that has been involved in a fatal crash with the driver dead...reading off of his driver's license, his name appears to be Arash...we found this telephone number on the driver and wanted to let you know..."

My heart dropped, I lost sense, and collapsed into a chair, shaking from head to toe. Moments later, I gasped for air, rose, and ran out of the house, not knowing where to go or what to do. I was at a loss. Somehow, I frantically rushed to my sister's house next door.

When Fataneh saw me in that state of panic and was told of the strange phone call, she tightly held my shivering body in her arms and kept saying,

"Wait. Calm down. Get a hold of yourself. Why do you believe a stranger? Let me make a few phone calls...to find out the truth."

She pulled me back into the house and seated me on a chair. I was sobbing uncontrollably when she called Arash's girlfriend,

"Hi...is Arash there?"

"Well yes, he's right here," she said.

"Arash is at his girlfriend's. See? I told you," Fataneh screamed.

"I have to speak to him myself," I yelled back.

"Hello...Dearie...are you OK...? Thank God. Thank God," I blurted while a torrent of tears was streaming down my face. But they were tears of joy.

Our shameless guest, bereft of basic human decencies, with the sole purpose of avenging himself against me, had devised that diabolic plot in retaliation. I was haunted by his horrid scheme for some time, shivering with fear, every time I thought about it.

A few months hence, my house guest and her beautiful, chubby baby left us too. Incidents like this and many more began to further sow the seeds of discontent and incubate the thought of divorce in my mind once again. I felt with my husband gone, most of my troubles would be gone too. My children were also in accord with me. His behavior had taken its toll on them as well. They were also tired of all the cacophony and tension that he created, and craved for peace.

***

"Heart has reasons, the mind knows nothing of...,"
~ Blaise Pascal

I, therefore, instigated the divorce proceedings. When Shahrokh was informed of an impending divorce, his initial reaction was,

"What? A divorce? How dare you? Not in a million years can you divorce me. Who are you to have the audacity to divorce me? It won't happen. Not in my lifetime. Do you wanna bet?"

Fortunately, we had left that patriarchal culture where men ruled unrestrained and bullied their wives undeterred, where divorce laws favored men over women. There, initiating and consummating a divorce by a woman, especially after the Islamic Revolution, was no less a herculean effort. Divorce pleadings by women were heeded by judges only in rare cases. There, men generally reigned unrestrained. And that was what my husband was used to. I knew in my heart that I was right in seeking a divorce and that God was on my side.

I hired a divorce attorney and related my life story and grievances to him in detail. After he made sure I had made up my mind, he drew and filed the divorce petition, and hence I was easily granted a divorce by a judge. Today, I am at peace with myself for having divorced Shahrokh. After all, before I divorced him, I had given him a second chance by bringing him back to America. Today, I have a clear conscience and no regrets.

After the divorce was effectuated, naturally one of us had to leave the house, and that was to be me.

I rented an apartment near where I worked and moved there. The second night after I had moved in, as I was falling asleep, I noticed a man standing to the side of my bed, hovering over me with a shiny object in his hand. I caught his wrist in time and screamed for help from the top of my lungs. After having been dragged on the floor some distance, which badly scraped my knees on the carpet, the intruder swiftly ran out and disappeared into thin air. After he escaped, I was still shaking and yelling, asking for help, but no one came to my aid. I stood vigilant till daybreak, and then shaken and distraught, I drove home.

My children were moonstruck with fear when they saw me pale, shaken, and disheveled. After I recounted the horrid incident, they insisted that I should stay with them and asked their father to leave the house instead. He left Houston for Austin, where someone he knew had secured him a job at a shop that sold Persian rugs.

With Shahrokh gone, the badly needed peace and normalcy returned to our home. But my relatives and friends who had only seen his fun side were perturbed by the breakup and his departure. They missed a pal who was ever ready to play a game of backgammon or cards for hours on end or to join in drinking sprees. They were the same ones who always envied me for having married such a fun guy. Even my sister Fataneh who had fond memories of her childhood with him, admonished me for having divorced him,

"How could you do such a thing? How could you bring yourself to throw him out at his old age?"

Little did they know of all my domestic troubles, and all that passed with Shahrokh under our roof.

A number of disjointed thoughts come to my mind. I remember my youngest sister, Firoozeh. She bore a boy, Sassan, and later, a girl, Shekoofeh. Sassan is an attorney now, and Shekoofeh is an interior designer.

Firoozeh, who mostly keeps to herself, did not pass any judgment one way or the other regarding my separation.

Our visas come to mind. The saga surrounding our Permanent Residency status did not cease to haunt us. Our visas were investor visas that had to be periodically renewed which, considering the ever-souring relations between Iran and America, was worrisome, lest it was denied.

Some of our relatives who had previously applied for political asylum suggested that route to us as a way to obtain Permanent Residency in America, but I was not too keen on that remedy. After a long time, with much difficulty and with the aid of an able, pricy attorney, I was finally able to obtain the U.S. Permanent Residency.

Lastly, it was during this time that due to the dreadful incident at my apartment and the consequent move back to our house, I missed a few days of work. And because of that, I sadly lost my job at Pala Royal.

***

"We are like the lyre which thou plucketh...,"

~ Rumi

Third Venture - Apparel Boutique

*"I wanted to live deep and suck out all the marrow of
life, to live so sturdily & Spartan-like as to put to rout
all that was not life, to cut a broad swath & shave
close, to drive life into a corner & reduce it to its
lowest terms...,"*

~ Henry D. Thoreau

Through a friend, I had come to know an American retailer who was in the apparel business. He was planning to open a boutique in San Antonio, selling women's clothing. He offered me to join him as a 50-50 partner, and I accepted. Regretfully, our business agreement was not inked, and it was only based on word of mouth. We verbally agreed that, on top of half of the yearly profit that the shop was to generate, I would receive a salary for working and managing the store.

I moved to San Antonio subsequent to our verbal agreement and rented an apartment in a reputable residential complex and began managing a small boutique in Alma, a well-known area.

My partner rented the space. He next ordered the racks and the hangers for hanging the clothes on for display. Soon after, he began to order and ship the merchandise, which I tagged with prices and hung on the racks to sell. I occasionally hired a helping hand too.

Unlike large department stores such as the likes of Macy's, with many of the same items in stock, we carried unique items and few in numbers. My partner never disclosed where he purchased the clothes he sent me, but it was clear that you could not find them anywhere else, like in a mall. I have still kept a skirt and a blouse from my time managing that boutique. They are silk, lightweight, wrinkle-free, and of high quality. And that was what that small store offered: unique, one-of-a-kind women's apparel.

And that was why it was popular among the tourists.

Alma was a suitable location for our boutique. It was near the city center, filled with sprawling shops and restaurants, and with proximity to the historic tourist site of the River Walk in the middle of downtown San Antonio. I kept the store open seven days a week. Weekends were considerably busier than weekdays due to the traffic generated by visiting tourists. All was going well. I was managing a thriving business I liked. I had a nice apartment, a car, and a decent paying job. And I was happy.

It was a small store. The cash register was placed on top of the checkout counter to the right side of the front entrance. I usually kept my purse and some food under that counter too.

One Sunday, a group of decent looking girls, seemingly tourists, well attired and well groomed, entered the store and browsed to the right and to the left. No one could have guessed they were shoplifters. I was working alone on that day and, apparently, they had noticed that. A few of them, aiming to divert my attention away from the checkout counter, inquired about prices of apparel on the far end of the store. Their companions, who were loitering by the front counter, having noticed my Gucci bag, took it without me noticing. Then they all left the store together in a jiffy.

I did not know what had occurred. I was still puzzled by their whirl-like entry and sudden departure. Soon, yet too late, I realized that my bag was missing. All that had transpired began to gradually sink in and make sense. But having been clad decently, I least expected such foul play by those women.

Later, when I would in between my ventures be taking temporary jobs at large department stores, such as Macy's, Dillard's, and Pala Royal, I would come to learn that shoplifters normally wear expensive clothing and flashy jewelry for deception. But at that time and place I had no such knowledge. What happened to me was a painful experience, more than I could bear.

My car keys, apartment keys, store keys, telephone book, credit cards, cash, driver's license, a Parker pen that I kept in memory of my father, and a few other things were gone. It was a Sunday afternoon. I did not know what to do. I felt the world had crashed on me. The only telephone number that I knew by heart was my daughter's, so I called her, devastated and in tears,

"Hi Dear...something awful has just happened to me. Some shoplifters stole my bag. I had everything in it...I don't know what to do."

My faculties had failed me. I could not think straight. My partner in Beverly Hills, California owned an apparel shop close to a photo shop where my daughter, ever since she had moved back to the US, was working at. She tried to calm me down,

"Please, don't panic. I'll tell your partner and I'll ask him to call you."

I kept thinking to myself, "How can I go home now? I don't even have my apartment keys. How can I lock up the shop?"

My partner called and tried consoling me. He suggested that I should immediately call a key maker and have keys made for the shop, and I did so. I had no money to pay the key maker, so I asked if I could pay him the following day, and he graciously agreed.

Then in the hope of finding the items that were of no value to those vandals, yet immensely critical to me, I even desperately searched in the nearby garbage bins, with no avail.

I caught a ride home by a neighboring shopkeeper. Upon arrival, I had to ask the building security guard to open my apartment door with his master key. Once home, I had to spend hours on the phone, calling my credit card companies to report the theft and have them cancel my cards. I had to obtain a driver's license anew. I kept pondering,

"How soon can I make up for all the things I have lost?"

And the next day I had to be at work, and in good spirits too.

How could some people be so inhumane? With no conscience?

The stress that this incident caused was to be the harbinger of an excruciating illness. A month had no sooner passed than I came down with a bad case of shingles. Those who have suffered from this disease can appreciate how painful it can be. What made it worse was that I was all alone and had no one to take care of me. I, all by myself, had to frequent a physician and have the prescriptions filled, all the while twisting in unbearable pain.

After about a year and a half of managing the store singlehandedly, I asked my partner for an accounting, so I could be paid my share of the yearly income, as we had earlier discussed. He only turned a deaf ear to my request. Upon my further insistence, he curtly said,

"Look, if you don't want to continue, you can have your initial investment back and leave."

And I did just that. Having lacked a written agreement, I had no other options. He could have not paid me anything after all. He might also have felt compelled to pay back my money only to save face with our mutual friend who had first introduced us, I could not be sure. I only thought,

"It's always best to stop your bleeding and cut your losses."

My partner chose not to honor the 50-50 partnership and its related benefits, foremost among them, sharing in the yearly profit generated by the store that he had originally agreed to. He had blatantly taken advantage of me by using my capital to purchase merchandise and sell at a profit that he alone pocketed. A native American would have probably brought a lawsuit against him, but being an immigrant and still not quite sure of my legal standing in the society, I chose to look the other way.

Time and again, I have noticed that those who have chosen honesty as their guiding light assume others to be the same. But sadly, it is often not the case. It is a pity how some of us mortals lose perspective in this ephemeral life we are living. We forget that to live in time is to die in time. No matter how much we hoard, we end up leaving it behind. Worse yet if the hoarding is done unethically, at the expense of someone else's lot. I believe the swindler swindles himself in the end because there will be a day of reckoning.

***

"You cannot do wrong without suffering wrong...,"

~ *R. W. Emerson*

Mansfield Dam Park

"All the rivers run into the sea, yet the sea is not full. From whence where all the rivers come, thither they return again...,"

~ *Ecclesiastes*

One summer day, we set off to Austin to visit Mansfield Dam Park, the large lake that Austin is famous for. We rented a large boat, and after having worn life jackets, we sailed on the ostensibly benign lake that laid behind the monstrous dam.

The boat we sailed on was abruptly stopped and some of the occupants, including Arash and Houshang, jumped into the water and began to swim. Someone, whom I could not quite make out, suddenly pushed me out of the boat too. Having had the bitter experience of my childhood near-drowning incident still fresh in my memory, I panicked and began to drown. With the dam incessantly pouring out excess water through its safety openings, the water current kept moving in the direction of the dam, pulling me along with it.

I heard someone in the boat who had noticed me drowning, yell,

"She is drowning...she is losing control...help her!"

Arash, having noticed my plight, swam toward me. Once he reached me, he kept pushing me toward the boat, but the current was pulling the water and me with a greater force in the opposite direction, toward the dam's precipice, with no respite. It seemed the more he tried to push me toward the boat, the less he was overcoming the opposing current.

After exerting much effort which took a long time, seeming like a lifetime, he was finally able to push me near the boat, where I was barely able to reach a rope that was thrown at me to grab. I clung to the rope with difficulty and was pulled out of the water to safety with the aid of four people inside the boat. This would be the epic remembrance of my Austin outing! The event to be remembered for a lifetime!

This third drowning incident was so horrifying that it left yet another indelible imprint on my mind. To this day, I am afraid of water. I am even afraid of a full bathtub.

Upon my return to Houston from San Antonio, I began to methodically research for a viable business to invest in. Among those I looked into were a printing shop, a travel agency, a coffee shop, a hair salon, and a small grocery store.

Experience had taught me that due to the lack of job security and future advancement, it was best to shun working for others. Instead, it would be more desirable if I ventured into a business of my own. Although, single-handed as I was, operating a business all by myself would be far from easy.

My college credentials in interior design, although accredited, did not help in securing a job either, because ample work experience was required.

But I never for a single moment ceased to be an optimist and was always ready to give all I had in me to working hard in any decent venture that came my way.

By this time, Arash together with Houshang had decided to open an auto repair shop, for which I loaned Arash the initial capital he needed. Unfortunately, they could not make it in that business and had to close down their shop after a couple of years, and my investment capital was henceforth lost too.

During this time, we continued to socialize with our extended relatives who resided in other states. One such family had a daughter, whom Arash befriended and fell into an amorous relationship with that finally ended up in their marriage. With family and friends who lived in other states in attendance, a glamorous and memorable wedding was arranged by the bride's mother in New Orleans. My daughter, Setareh, who had returned to the U.S. from Australia, attended the wedding too, before going to California. She, having been an expert in photography, put her talents to test on that day and bore the responsibilities of a professional wedding photographer.

***

"Love & you shall be loved...,"

~ *R. W. Emerson*

After their marriage, the couple rented an apartment in Houston and started living there as newlyweds.

They now have two sons, Aria and Kousha. Aria has married since, and is a father to a baby girl, which has made me a great-grandmother! Kousha is studying to be an engineer and will soon start living his independent life too. They are happily living as a family, which is a source of comfort and satisfaction for me. I can never forget those turbulent days when, painstakingly and with tooth and nail, I facilitated Arash's immigration to America. And now, seeing that he has formed a happy family together with his wife Rosana, a great wife and mother, gives me immeasurable delight.

Nephew, Hourang - Wedding

*"Nothing was greater than the quality of robust
love...it led the rest,"*

~ Walt Whitman

*"Gaze, till gazing out of gazing grew to being her I
gaze on, she & I no more, but in one,"*

~ Jami

My dearest nephew Hourang, Fataneh's younger son, was only three years old when he first set foot in America. After graduating from a medical school in El Paso, Texas as a general surgeon, he met a physician colleague, a surgeon also, whom he fell in love with and married.

Once I heard the good news, Hourang's life went through my mind like a motion picture. I thought about how he escaped death as an infant when he was afflicted with a respiratory infection. I remembered how tightly I held him in my arms, boarding that small airplane. Then my thoughts went back to when I strongly urged his father to immigrate to America. And how worried I was. If their move did not end up auspiciously, I would have had to shoulder the blame. I was happy in the extreme that I had played an active part in my nephew's success in life. And now at the news of his pending marriage, I was overjoyed from head to toe.

The not much less than magical wedding was held in the lovely Grand Cayman, one of the three serene islands in the western Caribbean Sea, collectively known as the Cayman Islands, an autonomous British Overseas Territory, requiring an entrance visa to visit.

The accommodations, and the many events that the wedding entailed, were arranged and managed by a professional team that among other things included booking flight tickets for the attendees, making hotel accommodations, wedding rehearsal, wedding ceremony, reception, food, and music. We flew in the day before the wedding, and the ceremonies got underway that same night.

Fardad, my other nephew, who had just flown in from Iran, surprised us with his unexpected and immensely joyful presence. The first night was spent by the families of the couple making acquaintances, delivering heartfelt speeches, citing childhood remembrances of the bride and groom, and expounding on their particular traits with hilarity.

Then a rehearsal of the wedding ceremony was conducted in minute detail. It included the procession (walking down the aisle), officiant's opening remarks, addressing the couple, the exchange of vows, the ring exchange, the pronouncement of marriage, the kiss, the closing remarks, and the recessional (walking back up the aisle).

Love melts the seemingly unconquerable barriers and removes them from one's path—it makes possible the impossible.

When the time for cutting the wedding cake comes, Iranian wedding ceremonies usually feature a special traditional dance by a number of close relatives of the bride and the groom. While holding a knife in hand, these individuals, one at a time, dance to the music and approach the bride to give her the knife, but tease her instead and pass the knife to another person, who continues the dance and repeats the antic. This goes on several times until the knife is finally handed out to the bride and the groom, who jointly, hand in hand, cut the cake.

Because of its uniqueness, I wanted this act to be added to the list of events that special night. After explaining the "knife dance" to Hourang, I insisted that he should include it in the festive events, but he said it was up to the event manager to decide, so I pleaded with the bride, asking her to add it to the list of events. Having liked the idea, she readily consented, and the event manager complied with this additional request, which turned out to be a different and exciting show to watch, especially for the American guests, who were seeing it for the first time, and they seemed to thoroughly enjoy it. It further enlivened the wedding ceremony with a jolly twist. The event manager had earlier asked me about the music to be played during the dance. I, having anticipated the question, pulled a CD from my purse. The instrumental musical played by Bijan Mortazavi, a renowned Iranian musician, brought everyone to their feet, dancing along enthusiastically.

The wedding was glamorous and dazzling, to say the least. Live music played both Iranian and American music with zeal, to which the guests danced enthusiastically.

Today, Hourang and Rebecca are happily married and have three bright daughters. Rebecca quit her job as a surgeon to allow her time to raise her children, which is a commendable sacrifice to make for a successful practicing physician. After having stayed home, raising her girls, she was offered a job in Tennessee a few years ago, which she could not refuse. I am proud of her and profoundly admire her.

I cannot think about Hourang without thinking about his older brother, Arzhang, six years his senior. He has not married yet and is living with his girlfriend. One of the unfulfilled wishes of my life is to see him married and have children of his own. He says he is happy living with his girlfriend, and besides, it is too late for him to have children at his age.

Arzhang is exceedingly warm and sociable. When he lived in Utah, he invited all of us to vacation at Park City, the premier ski resort in Utah, where one morning we all had a memorable brunch and afterwards tried the slopes.

Much to our surprise, he had already bought everything that was needed to ski, and in different sizes too. On the morning of the outing, he showed us a heap of ski paraphrenia, in multiple sizes, in the middle of the room and asked us to choose the ones that best fitted us: ski jackets, pants, socks, base layers, mid layers, gloves, neck warmers, goggles, helmets, boots, ski sticks, and skis. I asked myself, who would do such a thing? And the answer is, only someone who is passionate about family.

When Arzhang moved to Palm Springs, California, I visited him twice there. We spent some quality time together during my stay. I cooked some of his favorite dishes for him. We went to the movies together. And I helped decorate his new home. We also drove to San Diego together to visit his cousin and her family.

On another day, we drove to Los Angeles to shop at the Mikasa Chinaware Store. There, a pair of beautiful blue vases caught my eyes. I thought to myself that if I lived there, I would definitely buy them for myself. He must have read my thoughts because after I had gone back home, one day I received a box at my door. I opened it and saw those same vases I had cherished that day! I still have the vases, fitted into the rest of my decoration items–a great reminder of Arzhang – and I feel proud of him each time I see them.

On another occasion, when visiting a museum in Washington D.C., he had noticed a designed poster of a page out of the Quran. Knowing that I have a special inclination toward the Holy Scriptures, he had thought of me, and had bought and sent me the poster. I was elated to receive it. I framed it, and it has stayed singularly as my favorite tableau on my living room wall and again reminds me of my caring nephew each time I look at it. To this day, I think to myself, "Who can be this thoughtful except for Arzhang?"

I have always been proud of my nephews Hourang and Arzhang. They are endowed with exceptional kindness and impeccable integrity.

Scattered Family

*"Two roads diverged in a yellow wood, & sorry I
could not travel both...,"*

~ Robert Frost

My niece Pooneh has always loved her brothers passionately, a love that
has been more like an unconditional love, rare among siblings. I
remember she used to lavish them with pricy brand name gifts. I would
ask why she had to buy such expensive brand name items when she could
buy the same things much cheaper elsewhere. She would always say,
"They are my brothers and I love them and they deserve nothing but the
best." Whenever their parents were traveling to Iran, she would keep a
close, protective eye on her brothers, much like a parent.

Once Arzhang graduated from the medical school, he started practicing
medicine in Salt Lake City and asked his sister to help him in setting up his
practice there, and she gladly complied. After having lived in Atlanta,
Georgia for a short time, my dear niece moved to Utah. She purchased a
house in Utah and paid a moving company to move her furniture and
belongings there. Much to her chagrin, the moving company turned out
to be a sham and was never heard of again after they picked up her
belongings, and she lost all her household goods. Despite the fact that
she filed a police report, the perpetrators were never caught. It seemed
they were professionals and had well covered their tracks. Also, in those
days the technology was not as advanced which might have been a
contributing factor for not being able to catch them. After Pooneh lost
her belongings, the only thing that she brooded over was the loss of the
family photo albums because she thought them irreplaceable.

After about a year of living in Utah, Arzhang saw it more suitable, as a
cosmetic surgeon, to move to Palm Springs, and consequently made the
move, but Pooneh, who had come to like Utah, decided to stay behind.

In Utah, Pooneh purchased an old house, which she has since converted to a health spa. The house has a beautiful, verdant garden, where she has planted fruit trees, herbs, and flowers of different variety. She has a special affinity for nature. She, graciously, from time to time packs and sends me samples of her fruits in abundance so I can distribute them among other family members.

She continues to amaze me with how resolute she has been in life. As mentioned before, she had been another driving force behind her family's migration when she was an adolescent. And she has continued to prove at every turn that she truly is a self-made person.

At the time, Arzhang lived in Palm Springs, Pooneh lived in Salt Lake City, and Hourang lived in Atlanta.

My sister Firoozeh and her husband Hamid had moved to Atlanta. In the hope that other family members, who were scattered around in Texas, Utah, and California, would follow me, they encouraged me to join them there.

***

"Afoot & light-hearted, I take to the open road...,"

~ Walt Whitman

Therefore, at her insistence, I decided to move to Atlanta. I packed all of my belongings and arranged for a reputable moving company to have them insured and shipped to Atlanta.

Then I set off to Atlanta from Houston, driving alone in my brand-new Honda, following AAA maps. I always bought brand new cars before experiencing financial difficulties, past which I began to buy fine used cars, and I am satisfied with them just the same.

I had earlier asked my sister and son to accompany me on this trip, but since they could not, I took to the road alone, my favorite cassettes playing as I drove. On my long journey to Atlanta, I stopped in New Orleans and stayed the night at Badri's (my son's mother-in-law; Rosana's mother; also, my father's cousin), and continued on the next morning to Atlanta. I sometimes wonder how different driving was in those days without a cell or a GPS. Things have certainly changed a lot. But while speed and efficiency have improved, life is lived at a much dizzier pace. It has become much like a racing game. Sometimes it is as if everyone is bustling for the sake of bustling. Distances between family members have also grown, making face to face contacts a rarity. Thus, the warmth and the joy of family gatherings is sadly missing.

***

"Our journey is to the Rose-Garden of Union…,"

~ *Rumi*

Once in the vicinity of Atlanta, I got lost cruising along I-285 and had to stop at a gas station to call Firoozeh for directions. After endless driving, I finally reached her house. She had rented a spacious house with a separate wing to accommodate me. My belongings arrived a few days later.

Fourth Venture – 1st Dry Cleaning

"The question, O me! so sad, recurring...what good
amid these, O me, O life?
Answer: That you are here...that life exists &
identity... that the powerful play goes on & you will
contribute a verse...,"

~ From 'O Me! O Life!'

Before I decided to once again start a business of my own, I sojourned with Firoozeh for some time. After much analyzing, I arrived at the conclusion that a dry-cleaning store would be a suitable and safe trade for me. I particularly liked the fact that a dry-cleaning store was governed by stringent control measures. With each clothing item tagged and accounted for, I felt that unlike other businesses, the chances of theft by employees would be almost nonexistent.

The tale of the first invention of this trade is fascinating. The story goes that this trade dates back to the time of the ancient Romans, given that fragments of dry-cleaning shops were buried in the ruins of the city of Pompeii. But more recently, in the early 19th century, Jean Baptiste Jolly of France is reputed to have been the father of modern dry-cleaning. Legend has it that in 1825, when a clumsy maid had knocked over a lamp, spilling turpentine over soiled tablecloth, he had noticed the stains disappearing once the cloth was dried. Thus, using this method to clean clothes, he had opened the first dry-cleaning shop in Paris.

Around the same time, a freed slave by the name of Thomas Jennings, a tailor in New York, had registered a patent for a process called "dry scouring." He had then made a fortune dry-cleaning his customers' clothes, and with the new-found money, he had been able to buy his wife and children out of slavery!

And I felt I was destined to walk a path to fortune through dry-cleaning too! But my children voiced their concerns regarding my new undertaking. They believed dry-cleaning was an arduous business. Others also told me tales of failures in this business. They told me how two families had lost their life savings in this business. But I stayed determined and nothing could shake me.

I decided to first work at a dry-cleaning store so that I could learn all there was to know about the trade. After learning the ropes,, I would search to find a suitable location. Finding a location proved to be a difficult job. But with the help of a real estate agent, I finally was able to find a good location in a decent shopping center in Clarkston, Georgia.

The task that lay before me was an overwhelming one, no less. Among other things, it involved negotiating a lease with the landlord, negotiating equipment prices and terms of sale with the company that manufactured the equipment. Then there was the ordering of the cleaning supplies and detergents and hiring and training of the staff.

The equipment differed from the ones I had worked with during my short stint in a dry-cleaning store. But once they arrived and were installed, I was adequately trained to use them.

Additionally, I had to regularly frequent an attorney whose advice I sought in forming a new corporation, applying for and obtaining the necessary licenses, such as business and sales, and hiring personnel.

Those pre-opening tasks were cumbersome and time-consuming. It took a few months for everything to line up and be completed.

Then time came to open the shop. I knew I needed someone by my side, whom I could trust, and whose support I could rely on, and that happened to be none other than my daughter. I asked her if she could lend me a helping hand and she readily accepted as she had done before when I needed her. This time, she left Beverly Hills for Clarkston, Georgia, only for my sake. Her sacrifice in making the drastic move was akin to having someone forgo heaven for hell!

This was the second time she was bailing me out. The first time was when she quit school and joined me in California, helping me in running the grocery market. I felt enormously blessed for having such a daughter.

We rented an apartment in the vicinity of the dry-cleaning shop and began a life of intense work that the business demanded.

Sometimes, when spent and exhausted from working long hours, Setareh would turn to me and mockingly remark,

"Well, Mrs. Office Manager of the Ministry of Health, what are you doing here, working in a dry-cleaning shop?"

***

> *"These are the days that must happen to you...,"*
>
> *~ From 'Song of the Open Road'*

She was right in a way. But it did not apply to life in America. Here in this country, a different mode of working and living rules. It stems from its unique endemic culture. It is a demanding one indeed. One has to get acclimated to it. But here, irrespective of their stature in society, people work all legitimate jobs and trades. Here, you have a caste-free society. Back in Iran, civil servants and technocrats, as part of a higher caste, would shy away from working as shopkeepers.

Quite often, to shake the tension of the tedious work and to restore our spirits, we ventured into sight-seeing and hiking at the nearby historic Stone Mountain Park. This proved to be instrumental in rejuvenating us, both physically and mentally.

Interesting things happened at work, too, that lightened us up at times. For instance, I have a notorious habit of sneezing with a loud noise. One day, I let out just one of those boisterous sneezes, and an employee, who was working alongside Setareh, told her,

"What a loud sneeze?"

Setareh had returned,

"Yes. But, did you know that anyone who sneezes like that will have their good health guaranteed for three days?"

A few days later, I happened to sneeze raucously again, and the same employee was at it again,

"Well, I think with that sneeze, she'll have her health guaranteed for the next three years!"

Thinking of that apt response always brings laughter to me!

Sometime later, a nude dancing club opened for business at one end of the shopping center. During the day, the shopping center started to be jam-packed with cars when the club was open. People frequented that club nonstop, even during lunch hours, enjoying drinking and watching nude women dancing. That rowdy club began to be nothing but a headache for the merchants in the shopping center. I was puzzled to see how avaricious men were so keen to see naked women while I do not think women have such a burning desire to see naked men.

One morning, I saw a man, motionless, stretched out on the ground by the shopping center's dumpsters. I immediately called and informed the police. They quickly arrived and examined the body. He happened to be a drunkard, fast asleep. When the cops shook him, he woke up. One of the cops inquired,

"What are you doing here?"

He mumbled,

"I was at the club last night till late, and when I arrived home, my wife wouldn't let me in and told me to go back to where I'd been, so I came back tired and had to sleep here!"

One day, as I was driving to buy cleaning materials for my store, I happened to become the victim of a hit-and-run accident by a car, driven by some youngster. After the horrific collision, my car was pushed on to a rising mound by the road and stood slanted. The door on my side had been hit hard, and no matter how hard I tried, it would not open.

A driver approaching me from the other side, witnessing the accident, stopped and pulled me out from the passenger side and called the police. Once the police arrived, he explained all that he had seen. He had even been able to write down the license plate number of the perpetrator's car, which he handed out to the police. After a few months, the culprit was found. He happened to be a young lad who did not even own the car he had driven that day.

The car had no insurance either. But since I had full insurance coverage, my car was replaced with a brand-new one at no additional cost to me.

On the day of the court hearing, I was happily surprised to see the man who had come to my aid on the day of the accident. Apparently, he had been asked by the police to appear in court as a witness. It goes to show the admirable nobility of some Americans, and the extent to which they go in dispensing their civic duties. I do not know what I would have done had he not miraculously arrived at the scene of the accident, pulling me out of that perilous position in that pent-up car, and yet again, he had graciously come to my aid in court as a witness, like a guardian angel.

We continued to work hard in the dry-cleaning shop. But unfortunately, walk-in customers were not as many as I had hoped. Therefore, I engaged a pick-up-and-delivery laundry service to boost the sales. This worked out well until they dropped us one day with no rhyme or reason. This unexpected loss, coupled with the hassles the disruptive nude club had created, prompted me to think of selling my dry-cleaning shop.

After I sold my shop, I began working as a loan broker, helping folks secure mostly mortgage loans from banks. Setareh also began working in a time-sharing company, where people shared in the "time ownership" of an apartment at a tourist resort spot for a few weeks a year. This concept of vacation home sharing started when resort condominium units were built by real estate developers across America from coast to coast in the locations most desired by the tourists, and in which multiple parties hold rights to use these properties and are allotted their yearly period for usage.

But deep in my heart, I still wanted to open another dry-cleaning store, and so I remained on the look-out for a suitable location. Finding a good location for a dry-cleaning store is generally far from easy.

As a new shopping center begins construction, the developer starts advertising early on to lease the merchant spaces, often even before breaking ground. The location designated for a dry-cleaning shop is always highly sought after. In most cases, it is leased and assigned to a qualified merchant, years in advance of the completion of construction of a shopping center. As hard as the dry-cleaning business is, it is profitable and much in demand.

As mentioned before, one of the attractive features of this trade is that due to strict control measures and tagging procedures, employee theft is slim to none. And since the cleaning supplies are normally not subject to theft either, it is easier to control the money.

Having come to learn this trade, after I sold my shop, I remained inclined to open another one in the future.

Seekers are Finders

*"The world is a mathematical equation, which, turn it
how you will, balances itself...,"*

~ R. W. Emerson

Now, I would like to take the opportunity to elaborate on the spiritual awakening I experienced that put me on the path to seek the truth.

I was born and raised in a religious family and, by implication, had been seeking and praising my maker from time immemorial, but had not quite felt the spiritual awakening that I longed for.

After the Iranian revolution of 1979, the Islamic clerics seized power. Shortly after, they started executing the prominent figures of the old regime, among whom was an accomplished woman cabinet member, who had for a lifetime served her country, and for whom I had a great deal of admiration. She was put to death by stoning, nothing less than the height of barbarism.

Many members of the government and the military, all able, distinguished, and educated men, ended up before the firing squads as well.

When I heard about those atrocities, I turned to God. I said, "Dear Lord, if this is what Islam is all about, I do not want to be a Muslim, and if this is not the true Islam, please show me a sign."

I could not fathom how men of God could commit such atrocities in the name of Islam. Doubts about religion in general and Islam in particular were raised in my mind. And I set out to delve into a comprehensive study of religion.

I frequented churches, mosques, and *khaneghahs* (monasteries), but did not warm up to what I saw. I took part in religious congregations and listened to sermons, but saw hidden agendas, duplicity, and love for earthly possessions. I was not satisfied and stubbornly persisted in my quest for the truth, knocking on doors. I believe seekers are finders. Finally, in today's digital age, with the aid of mathematics, which in itself is a gift from God in rending veils, I was shown the traces of my Lord in the holy scriptures of the Quran, his last book revealed to humanity.

It all started this way: one day when I was attending a religious ceremony, I listened to an attendee deliver a lecture on Quran – expounding the mathematical significance of the Holy Book as advanced by a Quran scholar by the name of Rashad Khalifa. That speech was to have an everlasting influence on me. From that day on, I kept in touch with that lecturer, further exploring the groundbreaking views that she had spoken of. I then decided to put to test for myself all that she had claimed. I applied her mathematical litmus test to the two short Surahs of Nun and Ghaf in the Holy Book and saw for myself that it was true, the texts were bound, mathematically. I then thanked God for the long, sought-after revelation and began to follow the teachings of Rashad Khalifa.

The primacy of the Holy Scriptures as logos and symbols, and the traces of mathematics inherent in them, helped me understand and grasp the orderly governance of the universe, and thus the path to the truth was set before me. Mathematics, many believe, is the unspoken language of God, through which we humans can begin to grasp the truth. All that has a trace of the breath of the beloved in it, all the creation, including humans, vegetation, minerals, as well as the Holy Book, have makeups that are governed by mathematical laws.

This lifelong sought realization was the most grandiose gift ever bestowed on me. It was the dream of a lifetime come true. I then delved with bounteous zest into research regarding this subject that had always been close to my heart.

***

*"The more we lose ourselves in God the more we
find Him...."*

~ Rumi

Among those I studied was Galileo, the Italian natural philosopher, astronomer, and mathematician, who I realized, based on pure mathematics, without having access to modern computer technology, had an inkling to the mystery of the universe. Although, it has been interpreted that in the holy scriptures, in Surah 27, Ayat 82, reference has been made to this modern device.

I also came to learn how the mathematics inherent in the Holy Scriptures was first discovered by an Egyptian scholar by the name of Rashad Khalifa, whose name I mentioned, by a code in the Quran.

He set out to purge the man-made teachings that had found their way into Islam by the so-called guardians of the faith, thus corrupting it. He was a puritan who believed that the Islamic beliefs and practices should be based on the Holy Scriptures alone.

Starting in 1968, he had used the computer technology to analyze the frequency of letters and words in the Holy Book. He had, thereupon, detected a mathematical structure inherent in the Quran that renders it incorruptible. And that, he had claimed, was the proof of its divinity.

I also delved into studying the works of some of the notable scholars of the Quran, such as Dr. Maurice Bucaille, Dr. Gary Miller, and Dr. Gary Wills. They have also hinted at the grandiosity and incorruptibility of the scriptures. Dr. Gary Wills, a prolific writer of over 50 books, has written a book titled, "What the Quran Meant and Why It Matters," which is quite informative and a marvel.

Ever since this life-changing realization, I can feel God and His love in every fiber of my being, and as a consequence, I feel immensely blessed.

I feel connected to a higher plane of reality, the absolute, the Divine Throne, and I am energized and feel reborn with the love of God. When in need, time and again, God has come to my aid, for which I feel immeasurably blessed.

***

"Oh Lord, who did I forsake for these; they're not thee...,"

~ *St. Augustine*

Fifth Venture- 2nd Dry Cleaning

*"Soul...Lo, it was hurled midst the sign-posts &
ruined abodes of this desolate world. It weeps when
it thinks of its home & the peace it possessed...,"*

~ Avicenna

I continued searching for a location to open another dry-cleaning shop until I was finally informed by my real estate agent that a desirable location in a busy shopping center had become available.

A shop had closed down, making an ideal space available to rent. I hurried to consummate a lease agreement, which unlike the last time, went more smoothly. Since I had prior experience running a dry-cleaning store, I was spared some of the tedious hassles I had encountered the first time. Although, I still had to retain an attorney to help with the legal issues surrounding executing a lease, forming a corporation, and applying for the required licenses.

After scanning the equipment manufacturing firms across the country, studying their brochures, I located one that I liked. And after the customary negotiations, I signed a contract to purchase the needed equipment and to have them installed in a month. The landlord granted me four months of free rent from the date the lease agreement was signed. Therefore, after the equipment was installed, I enjoyed a period of three months of free rent while operating.

To draw customers, I put up a sign, advertising, "Dry Cleaning - Any Item - Only $2.99."

I knew this sign would attract a great many customers and it did. A flood of customers poured in with all kinds of dirty clothes, from dresses to overcoats.

When a friend, whom I had the pleasure of meeting in the Quran classes I attended, heard about my new venture, he offered to join me as a partner, and I gladly accepted. I was happy that I had a pious individual with high morals as a partner. I thought, both from a working and from a financial standpoint, a partner would alleviate some of the pressure this arduous trade imposed.

We officially commenced operation and opened our door to customers.

Based on my past experience, I knew that in a start-up business, to allow for work-in capital to build up, one invariably had to, for a few months at least, refrain from taking out a salary. A start-up-business requires bracing up during the critical initial period of operation, during which time one has to weather the storm. Drawing a salary should start only after a nascent business is well established and profitable. But my partner, much like most Iranians who start a business and milk it from day one and often fail due to draining the business of cash, insisted on receiving a salary from the start. I tried to reason with him, but he would not listen.

This inevitably led to friction between us from the outset.

Another problem I had with my partner was that he represented himself as the sole proprietor and once absent, the customers demanded to only see him: the owner of the establishment. This created unnecessary confusion.

I thought to myself that, with our budding differences from the start, it may not be wise to maintain this erosive partnership and saw it best to part ways with him before going any further. I, therefore, repaid him his investment capital, severed our business relationship, and continued to operate the shop by myself.

I rented an apartment near my store. I opened the shop to customers each day at seven o'clock in the morning. I had hired a few employees to tend to technical aspects of the business, such as operating and maintaining the equipment, pressing, and cleaning stains.

I stood at the front counter, greeting customers and answering questions. It was a hard business to run for a middle-aged woman, a foreigner, all alone, having to manage low caliber help. Meanwhile, I aimed to provide the best service to my customers. But being single handed, it was a tiring and corrosive affair.

Usually, in time of need, Setareh always stepped up, came to my aid, and saved me, but she had since been married to an American physician and could not lend her support anymore. She was also pregnant with a child and had to refrain from exposure to harmful cleaning products.

I had to perform tasks that were not fit for a woman, such as climbing a ladder to change fluorescent ceiling bulbs or cleaning a multi-ton washing machine. The dry-cleaning business has a unique system all unique to itself. To run it properly, much effort must be exerted each day in following certain critical regiments. As a perfectionist, I was exceedingly particular and aimed to provide my customers with the cleanest products, in the best timely manner.

Not before long, I came to be at odds with my employees who would not adhere to strict rules. They, for instance, did not show up at times. When called, they would return with a yawn,

"Oh, I'm tired today and can't work. Sorry."

An American male employer would probably fire such irresponsible employees on the spot, but I could not. It was not easy for me to consistently replace and recruit employees. They knew that, and took advantage of my shortcoming.

When my employees did not show up for work, I had to, all by myself, press, clean stains, and attach tags on clothing items. Working hours started at seven o'clock in the morning when all the other shops were still closed because our customers dropped off their clothes before they went to work.

One day, a customer brought in a seemingly pricy, light color overcoat that had badly been stained with ink. I did my best to remove the stain, but it was still faintly visible. Although in trying to clean the stain I had spent extra time, I did not charge the customer any more than the advertised $2.99. A few days passed, and one day, I received a registered legal letter from that customer, putting me on notice of a lawsuit she had filed against me.

I had to appear in the court of law over $2.99!

I showed up in court on the appointed day. The presiding judge inspected the overcoat and asked the woman plaintiff to state her case.

She showed the stain on the overcoat and complained that it had not been completely removed. Then the judge asked me to respond. I said I had not hesitated to put extra time and effort in removing the stain without charging extra, but all what remained was not removable. The judge turned to the plaintiff.

"You knew that this dry-cleaning shop charged only $2.99. Why didn't you take this fine overcoat to a more expensive dry-cleaning?"

He continued, quizzically,

"It looks like she has done her best to rid the coat of the stain. Had you paid her anything extra?"

The plaintiff responded with a quivering voice,

"No, your honor."

The judge turned to her again with an admonishing tone that spoke volumes,

"You have no right to file a complaint, ma'am. Case dismissed." Bang.

"Thank God," uttered I.

I was overjoyed and grateful for having appeared before a fair and sensible judge.

I continued working hard to the best satisfaction of my customers, and my business finally turned the corner, prospered, and began to generate a profit. But I was so exhausted from all the work that I felt I was compromising my health and could not even think straight due to all the fatigue.

My son Arash could not come to my aid, for he had no interest in such a trade. My daughter Setareh could not come to my rescue either, because she was pregnant with a child.

During this period, I was concurrently entertaining the thoughts of making a long-awaited pilgrimage to Mecca that is incumbent upon Muslims. Therefore, I decided to sell my business. I was so exhausted, both physically and emotionally, that I did not even think of keeping the business and hiring someone to manage the business in my absence.

Although the shop had begun to boom and generate a profit, I just wanted to rid myself of the business, no matter what. I guess once one is spent, money loses its significance, and keeping one's health gains more currency.

While I made the traveling plans for my epic journey, I put my shop up for sale. Two men, roommates, offered to buy my shop. I reached an agreement with them over the price and the conditions of the sale. We signed a "Buy and Sell" agreement, and I received a deposit. It was agreed that upon my return from Mecca, they would officially take over the shop, and I would train them for a period of two weeks.

They made a special request: they asked, instead of undergoing training after I returned, if they could, prior to my departure, start working at the shop to satisfy the training requirement, and I agreed. They started to arrive early each morning, and I, in minute detail, taught them all the nitty-gritty and the quirks of the trade.

I believe that God never leaves us alone in a time of need. It is the faith and trust in him that has sustained me during hard times. At the time, I felt immersed in his love and guiding light. I knew it was God who had saved me time and again. The following is only one account of how he saved me.

∗∗∗

> *"As I walk through the valley of the shadow of death,*
> *I fear no evil, for thou art with me...,"*
>
> *~ Psalms*

I had a woman in my employment, who worked the press machine. When I hired her, she asked me to refrain from withholding employee taxes from her paychecks. And she pledged to pay them herself at the end of the year. I complied with her request and had her fill out and sign the appropriate tax forms.

Tax season arrived, and one April morning before any shops had opened for business, as I opened my shop, I saw her approaching me violently, sticking her finger in my face, almost poking my eye, yelling viciously,

"Give me that paper!"

Dumbfounded and shivering, I asked,

"What paper?"

"The paper I signed," she screamed with a flushed face.

She suddenly leaped toward me, grabbed me by the throat, squeezing the airway, and began to choke me.

"Hurry, give me that paper, or I'll kill you."

Frozen to the bone, heart pounding, I managed to utter, faintly,

"It's not here. I gave it to my accountant."

Suddenly, the two purchasers arrived on the scene and sprang to intercede,

"Stop. What are you doing?"

***

> *"God reappears with all its parts in every moss and cobweb...,"*
>
> ~ St. Augustine

They separated her from me in a wild scuffle. I ran out to drive away, but that wicked lady rushed after me and grabbed me from behind with a strong grip before I could reach my car, and she would not let go. Those two men had to engage her again with all their might, pulling her away from me.

While I was fiercely shaking, I managed to quickly drive away. I could hear my own heart pounding hard, about to burst my chest. When I reached my apartment, I called 911 and gave the authorities an account of the incident.

From what appeared, that woman had gone to an IRS office to pay her taxes, and there, she had learned of the large sum she was liable to pay. She, apparently out of sheer desperation, had decided to come to threaten me, so that she could, by force, retrieve and destroy the tax form she had earlier signed. This would have shifted the tax liability onto my shoulders, and I would have had to pay her taxes.

After providing the police with the details, still shaking, I drove back to my shop but did not step out of the car for fear of yet another fracas. Finally, the police arrived and proceeded to speak to the woman employee. Once they finished talking, they approached me casually.

"You're lucky that those two guys arrived just in time, or else, that insane woman could've killed you," they said nonchalantly.

I pleaded anxiously, "Well. Now, what will you do about it?"

I could not believe what the officer said in response to my plea.

"Well. Now that she hasn't killed you, there is nothing we can do. Had it been any different, we would've charged and arrested her. But now, what can we charge her with?" he said matter-of-factly.

I was puzzled by their utter indifference. I even showed them my neck that was bloodshot by her fingers pressing it, to no avail. I could not believe that justice was not dispensed for what she had done to me. But I was grateful that my life was spared.

It seemed as if certain events worked in tandem to save me. After all, had I not agreed that the buyers start to work immediately, I would have probably been alone and subject to that woman's deadly assault. Death would not have been far-fetched at the hands of that belligerent woman, with no one around at that early morning hour.

I believe that there is a reason for everything and events are destined to unfold by levers that are in a higher plane of unseen reality. I also believe that once you enter into a covenant with God and abide by it, he will protect you.

***

"I am constrained every moment to acknowledge a higher origin for events than the will I call mine...,"

~ R. W. Emerson

I cherish the Godly love that never ceases to provide the most fitting solutions.

I then set off on my pilgrimage to Mecca to perform the Islamic ritual known as Hajj.

Here, I would like to say a few words about this ancient ritual. Hajj is an annual Islamic pilgrimage to Mecca, Saudi Arabia, the holiest city for Muslims. It is a religious duty for Muslims that must be carried out at least once in their lifetime by those who are physically and financially capable of undertaking the journey and can support their family during their absence. It is one of the Five Pillars of Islam. In a way, it is a demonstration of the solidarity of Muslims around the world, and of their submission to God and the tenets of Islam. The word "Hajj" means, "to attend a journey," which connotes both the outward act of a journey and the inward act of intentions. The rites of this holy pilgrimage are performed over a week, in the last month of the Islamic calendar.

The ritual of pilgrimage to Mecca is considered by Muslims to stretch back thousands of years to the time of Abraham. Interestingly, in ancient times, the pilgrimage was attended by Christians and Jews as well as Muslims. But today, the government of the Saudi Arabia has forbidden non-Muslims from attending these rituals. During Hajj, pilgrims join processions of millions of people, who simultaneously converge on Mecca for the week of the pilgrimage, and perform a series of rituals: each person walks counterclockwise seven times around the Kaaba, the cube-shaped building and the direction of prayer for Muslims, then trots back and forth between the hills of Safa and Marwah seven times, then drinks from the Zamzam Well, goes to the plains of Mount Arafat to stand in vigil, spends a night in the plain of Muzdalifa, and performs the symbolic Stoning of the Devil by throwing stones at three pillars—to rid oneself inwardly of evil intentions.

It is worth noting that not every annual Hajj pilgrimage has been a benign event. A number of fires and stampede related disasters have occurred in the past.

On April 15, 1997, a fire caused by explosion of canisters of cooking gas had erupted in the overcrowded tent city in Mina, a district a few miles east of Mecca, where an estimated two million Muslim pilgrims had gathered for the first day of Hajj. The fire had been fanned by high winds, causing the destruction of an estimated 70,000 tents, killing 217 and injuring over 1,200, many of whom had been trampled in the panic.

As late as, September, 24, 2015, an event described as a, "crush and stampede," had caused deaths of an estimated 2,400 pilgrims, suffocated or crushed, making it the deadliest Hajj disaster in history. The largest number of victims had been from Iran, followed by Mali and Nigeria. The crush had taken place on a road leading up to Jamaraat Bridge in Mina, where the Stoning of the Devil is performed. It was said that a group of pilgrims on buses were allowed to descend onto the pathways that lead to the bridge at a time that was not allocated to them, resulting in overcrowding of a narrow passage.

And when time came for my pilgrimage, fire yet again disrupted the events just before my arrival for the ceremonies at Mount Arafat, near Mecca—causing human casualties. Fortunately, I was not a witness to the fires engulfing the tents. The authorities had put them out the day before and covered the burnt tents with new tents by the time we arrived there—a day late. But the unpleasant smell of the smoke was still in the air. At the news of the incident, my daughter panicked, she later told me. Terribly worried, with much effort and after many calls to the local authorities, she was finally able to locate and talk to me to make sure I was unharmed. She was relieved once she heard my voice on the telephone.

Finally, I was happy and honored to have completed my coveted pilgrimage safely, and upon my return, I officially turned over the shop to the new owners. I lost a good chance in a viable business but had no other choice except to move on.

I remember during those days, Setareh, was pregnant with her child.

Daughter, Setareh

*"She walks in beauty, like the night of cloudless
climes & starry skies & all that's best of dark & bright
meet in her aspect & her eyes...,"*

~ Lord Byron

*"Strong is your hold, O mortal flesh! strong is your
hold, O love...,"*

~ From 'Leaves of Grass'

Setareh is uniquely simple and down to earth. She never sought fancy clothes, bags, make-up goodies, or other knick-knacks that girls her age cherished. She often shows up at parties clad in a simple pair of sports designer jeans and a T-shirt, without any makeup, and she always looked great and had many admirers. Her friends respect her for her lack of pomp, both in clothes and in demeanor. She had never been fond of glitz. Life's dazzles had always been devoid of appeal to her.

I, who had no say in my son's wedding, was inclined to compensate for it by throwing a glamorous wedding party for my daughter. But I was constantly faced with Setareh's objections, who shunned glamour. She neither wanted a sofreh aghd nor a wedding gown. I was left with no option but to plead with my future son-in-law for help. I sat with him uneasily, worried that he might not heed my advice either,

"Mark, Dearie, our tradition calls for a splendid wedding, going back a millennium. It is an old custom to spread a sofreh aghd that features a large mirror and two candelabras on each side, and other items that are emblematic of health and happiness and deemed good omen for your future married life together, such as honey, traditional baked sweets, herbs and cheese rolled in flat bread."

I said all this with passion, and not knowing how he would react. In the end, I sheepishly asked,

"So, what do you think?"

"Wow, this all sounds great. Please arrange all that you just explained. I love it," he said, beaming with a smile.

Mark took Setareh to the prominent Cartier store to buy her an expensive diamond ring. Refusing to buy a flashy ring, she had mockingly said,

"No way. I'm not a Christmas tree to be wearing a shiny object like that!"

She instead chose a simple wedding ring.

After Mark consented to the traditional wedding I had suggested, I sprang to action. First, I invited relatives and friends from California and Texas. Then I invited our local friends.

Next, I began to prepare for the wedding that I, for years, had longed for. I rented a large private party room and designated an area just for the sofreh aghd . I procured all the items that a traditional wedding spread needed, save for the mirror and the candelabras. Since the couple would permanently keep those special items, I felt they needed to choose them to suit their own tastes. I covered the floor with Persian rugs I had brought from Iran and designed the room as best I could.

I rolled feta cheese and fresh green herbs in unleavened flatbread, cut them to small pieces, and served them as finger food. I had different colored corsages made for the groom and the bride's family. I set them on a silver tray. The family members wore them upon arrival. I wrapped handfuls of *noghl*, a sweet Iranian delicacy, in small pieces of silk cloth and hung them from the branches of a small tree I had earlier set up in a corner. Next to it stood a round table filled piled high with seasonal fruits around a large pineapple, fringed with a plethora of beautiful fresh-cut flowers.

In addition to our local guests, relatives and friends poured in from all over including California, Texas, Louisiana, and even Iran. Also, my sister Fataneh, who had gone back home with her husband to visit her ailing mother-in-law, arrived alone from Iran. But her husband had stayed behind.

Shahrokh, who had moved from Austin to Gadsden, Alabama, where his nephew lived, was present to give away the bride. Pooneh, Arzang, and Hourang brought joy to our celebration with their presence. My sweet sister Firoozeh, and her children, and of course my son, Arash and his family, including his in-laws Badri and her husband, were in attendance as well.

Pooneh and our friends from California, Fozhan and Narges, were of great help to me in making the arrangements.

The wedding got underway magnificently. And I was satisfied with the arrangement I had made. It was a rather small wedding, yet a warm, jolly, and memorable one.

Setareh kept up complaining about the glitz I had infused into her wedding. But to placate her, I kept on reminding her with a grin,

"Look. This has nothing to do with you. This is all for Mark. He has asked me for a traditional wedding, and I'm complying with his wish."

She ended up not wearing a long wedding gown after all. Instead, she chose to wear a short and simple white dress. But at my insistence, she consented to wear a beautiful flower in her hair. Fataneh, who was a hair and make-up artist, insisted on applying make-up the way she normally would on a bride, but Setareh, much to her disappointment, refused and would not budge. Setareh, even without a formal bridal gown or a hair cover, looked wonderful and uniquely beautiful.

I had asked a good friend to administer the traditional oath of wedlock, as the officiant. Her remarks were embellished with recitations from the Holy Scriptures, sanctifying the holy union. After the formal wedding recitations came to an end, the gifts from the relatives and myself were presented to the couple on a silver tray adorned with fresh flowers.

After the formal wedding ceremony, the live band started playing Iranian and American music, enlivening the festive occasion. All went quite well and everyone had a wonderful time. I certainly did my share of dancing till late at night—something I love to do (I often dance when I am alone at home!)

The newlyweds set off to Greece for their honeymoon the day after the wedding. And since they had already purchased a house, while out of the country they asked me to stay in their new house.

On the second night following their departure, heart-pounding and sweating profusely, I woke up from a horrid nightmare. I often have a bad dream as a harbinger of some unforeseen tragic event. The dream I had worried me for the newlywed's safety. When I confided to Arash about my dream, knowing that my dreams usually came true, he got perturbed and, to make sure they were fine, he decided to locate the couple in Greece.

We did not know which hotel they were staying at, so he started calling the hotels in Greece at random. He was finally able to track them down at one of the hotels he called.

He began to ask mundane questions, such as how things were, and if they were having a good time. They were taken completely by surprise to receive a call at that early morning hour. They said all was great, and they were having a great time. After hanging up the phone, Arash turned to me, jokingly,

"Ah, see, they are fine and having a swell time on their honeymoon. A woman's dream never comes true!"

Unfortunately, although the dream would not apply to Setareh and Mark, that did not happen to be the case.

Brother-in-Law Dies

"For dust thou art, & unto dust shall thou return...,"

~ Genesis

*"O lovers, O lovers, it is time to abandon the
world...the drum of departure reaches my spiritual
ear from heaven...,"*

~ Rumi

A few days later, one very early morning that seemed like all the other early mornings, I jumped out of bed to the sound of the telephone ringing. I had not expected to receive a call that early in the day. My heart sank, and I had a premonition that something undesirable had happened. I picked up the phone with a racing heart to the sound of Pooneh, sobbing and shrieking, uncontrollably.

"Auntie, my father, my father..."

"What about him? What has happened? Tell me please."

"Auntie, he's dead...Auntie, he's dead..."

"What? How could it be? I just spoke to him over the telephone a couple of days ago. He was just fine. He congratulated me on Setareh' wedding. He said he wished he was here so he could make a video of the ceremonies. I can't believe it...How could this be?"

Houshang had died of a sudden cardiac arrest before the eyes of his ailing mother he had gone to visit. He was pronounced dead before he had arrived at the hospital.

Firoozeh and I immediately flew to Houston to be with the children, who had gathered there, to console them. We were all grief-stricken and in disbelief.

His sudden, untimely passing had a colossal adverse effect on all of us, devastating the collective family. Although grown-up by then, his three children were in a state of shock and distress for quite some time. I would find peace sooner than others though, and again, I credit my abiding faith for it.

***

"Death is a turning over from time to eternity...,"

~ William Penn

Houshang was still young, and his dying, especially in the presence of his ill mother, would have been horrifying and immensely difficult to witness.

But now that destiny had played its hand as such, there was nothing to be done. We had to collect ourselves and proceed prudently. Fataneh was to immediately fly over to Iran to take part in the extensive mourning services that would follow.

After she attended the services and the bereavement period ended, she proceeded with the legal matters surrounding her deceased husband's inheritance. She also needed her children to execute some legal papers.

Because of her children's lack of familiarity with Farsi and the Iranian laws, I had to take the lead and help.

Iranian law does not cease to uphold Iranian citizenship, even when one migrates to another country. Since they had left at a young age, they did not possess valid Iranian passports and new ones had to be issued before any inheritance requests could even be filed. And to obtain the passports, long forms had to be filled out in Farsi and current pictures needed to be taken.

I first had to request the forms from the Iranian Interest Section (de-facto embassy) in Washington. Then every day, working around their busy schedules and different time zones, I had to arrange the time to call each one, translate the questions from Farsi to English, ask the questions in English, receive the answers in English, translate them into Farsi and fill the questionnaires.

Once the forms were filled, I had to send them separately to each of the children for their signatures. Upon receiving the signed forms, I had to register-mail them back to the Iranian quasi-embassy to obtain an Iranian passport for each one of them before filing the inheritance petitions.

After they were issued valid Iranian passports, more forms, such as powers of attorneys and inheritance petitions, had to be filled out following the same routine, signed, and register-mailed to the Iranian Interest Section in Washington to officiate the inheritance, which all proved a tedious and time-consuming affair, no less.

Fataneh returned after a while, but this time, sadly, without her other half.

Since I was anticipating the next step, I had taken copies of each and every paper that I had filled at every step of the way. When she returned, I gave her a thick folder of the paperwork I had done for her children.

<u>Sixth Venture - Home Construction</u>

"Did he who made the lamb make thee...?"

~ *William Blake*

Once again, I was approached with a business proposition by another seemingly good friend, whom I had come to meet in the Quran classes I regularly attended. This friend, who appeared to be upright and pious, attended the classes with enthusiasm, which to me was a testament to his faith and veracity. I was particularly good friends with his wife, a most respectable lady. We often socialized. Sadly, years later, their marriage was to end in divorce. He, one day, suggested,

"I'm a civil engineer and can build houses, but have no capital to start on my own. Would you be interested in joining me as a partner? If you provide the initial investment, I'll pitch in my work and expertise. I will manage the construction, and once each house is sold, we'll equally share in the profit."

It sounded like a fair offer and I was delighted by it. After discussing it in detail, I expressed interest.

"Yes, I'm interested."

We sought legal advice from my attorney. A legal agreement was drawn and signed by the two of us. Additionally, since he had thus far neglected to execute a personal will, although he had been living in America for a number of years, one was drawn and executed by him as well. Our arrangement called for me to inject the initial capital. Since I was to be a silent partner and he would be managing the construction on a day-to-day basis, a monthly salary was to be awarded him. Once each house was sold, the profit was to be shared equally by the two of us.

To get started, we formed a Georgia Corporation and opened a corporate bank account, and I deposited the initial capital. After some months of waiting for the completion of the construction and the sale of the first house, one day I was shocked to find out that my partner had opened a separate bank account in his own name, and furthermore, had sold the first house and pocketed the proceeds without even telling me. I could not believe it. I held a meeting with him and expressed my anger,

"What have you done? Why did you open a second bank account behind my back? Why did you sell the house without telling me? Where is my share of the profit?"

He responded, shamelessly,

"Well, I don't think it's fair for me to spend all my precious time doing all the hard work and then give you half of the profit."

I recounted our deal,

"Firstly, you drew a monthly salary for the time you spent on the project. Secondly, it was I who put up the initial capital. What about our contract that you agreed to and signed? Was it not your offer on day one, for us to equally share in the profit? Did you not take out a salary? You didn't have any money to build a house, to begin with. It was my money that made it all possible. This is nothing but plain fraud."

He was unfazed and would not budge. Finally, after a long time, I received my exact initial investment and nothing more.

He, who had taken advantage of me by using my money in venturing into the home construction business, has by now amassed a sizable fortune and has since turned into a prominent real estate developer. Misdeeds as such, I believe, will eventually see a day of reckoning.

What disturbed me most was my own attorney's unexpected face-about, the same attorney whom I had over the years come to trust and rely on. He, who had since struck a close relationship with this infamous person, drawing numerous sales contracts for the houses he was selling, made a mockery of justice, shrugged me off, and with a cowardly turn-about, began to defend him,

"Well, you should be happy to be receiving the money you invested. I think you should move on. He could've paid you nothing, after all!"

He took his side. It seemed that he had been bought off.

After this bitter experience, I came to realize that not everyone who seems to be spiritually upright is genuine.

***

"Better a debauched canary than a pious wolf...,"

~ Anton Chekhov

With this heartbreaking experience, I can say that my investments did not pay off in two of my undertakings. First, it was the boutique business, where we had verbally agreed to a deal. There, I drew a monthly salary for my work. And next, it was with this man in the construction business, and despite a signed partnership agreement too. This is a testament to the fact that with an agreement or without, it sometimes does not make much difference if you are conned. And once you are conned, the difficult avenue to a legal remedy that requires time, money, and effort, may not be worthwhile.

I have always, with family, friends, or strangers tried to be honest and fair in my affairs and have, therefore, expected others to reciprocate in kind. But I have, through the hard way, learned that not all people are honest.

I did not divulge his dishonesty and misdeed with anyone in our spiritual study group and kept it to myself, lest his reputation be tarnished. Although, I was advised by family members to do otherwise and reveal his mischief.

It remains an unanswered question for me as to how one can truly gauge other people? Through extensive socializing? By their faith in God? Based on their amiable demeanor? Or their apparent honesty? But it seems that none of the above may be a viable yardstick when money is at stake.

Have some people no inkling that to live in time is to die in time? Do they forget that once they are gone, they leave all possessions behind?

After this ordeal, while waiting for a business opportunity to yet arise, I sought employment in various capacities for a few years. Ever since my younger days, I had always been used to being active in life.

Seventh Venture - Clinic

"The greatest happiness for the thinking person is to have explored the explorable & to venerate in equanimity that which cannot be explored...,"

~ Goethe

Sometime later, a physical therapist named Mathew, together with an Iranian friend, decided to open a physical therapy clinic. They offered me to join them too. We held a long meeting, where I had the pleasure of meeting Mathew, and after an extensive conversation, my interest was aroused.

I subsequently held a good number of meetings with Mathew to get a better feel for who I was partnering with, his capabilities, and the nature of the business he was advocating. This I did, particularly because I did not want to be yet again entangled with another undesirable partner, nor did I want to step into something that did not interest me. During those fact-finding meetings, Mathew came across as an honest person who knew his trade. Also, the prospect of helping others in need of treatment interested me. When I felt comfortable with Mathew and his mission, I accepted to be a part of his team.

The three of us put up equal sums of money and entered into a partnership. With Mathew's extensive knowledge and experience, a genuine physical therapy center opened its door to patients and began to operate.

This time, unlike other businesses that I had started, I did not have to worry about the initial set up. Mathew bore the brunt of finding the location, retaining an attorney, and consummating a lease with the landlord. He, further, arranged for the purchase of all the equipment and appliances that were needed.

215

I was assigned the tasks of receiving patients, keeping records, answering calls, and procuring the needed daily provisions. It was a good clinic. It gave me great satisfaction to see that our center was instrumental in helping others regain their health. But sometimes, as a witness to the plight of some dreadfully disabled patients, I could not help but be perturbed, and hence, peace was driven away from my mind for a long time.

For instance, we had a young, tall, and handsome patient by the name of Alex who had been, through no fault of his own, an unfortunate victim of an auto accident that had left him paralyzed for life. He had happened to be an unlucky passenger in a car driven by his friend when the accident had occurred. I was so disturbed by seeing young patients like Alex who had unluckily been victims of wretched accidents that I would lose sleep for countless nights.

Alex underwent daily intensive treatment. It took a year for him to be able to barely recognize and count numbers. He was severely paralyzed and could neither speak nor walk. He had literally turned into an immovable mound of meat that was barely alive. His family were devastated. They had turned their home into a makeshift hospital that could accommodate a quadriplegic. Every time his mother and sister brought him in for therapy, I shared in their misery, and with a sinking heart, shed tears with them, as if he was my own son. I felt like a member of their family.

We had other patients like Alex. But while I was disturbed by their atrocious conditions, I was happy that we could help improve their health, and somewhat alleviate their misery.

Time passed and our Iranian partner lost patience with the business, as it had not generated a profit yet. He thought of dumping his share on me and leaving the partnership. He began to talk about wanting to leave the country to visit his ailing mother in Iran, so he asked me to buy his share. After consulting with Setareh, she advised me to refrain from buying his share.

Our Iranian partner's impatience sowed the seeds of discord among us partners to the point when Mathew decided to shut down the clinic altogether. He said he could no longer continue operating a business that was imbued with discordance, tension, and bereft of peace of mind. One partner's lack of foresight finally resulted in the closure of a decent business.

However, in the end, Mathew turned out to be a fair and honest partner. After the partnership was dissolved, on top of the past due salary for my time working in the clinic, he graciously returned, over the course of six months, every penny I had invested, plus interest. After our separation, he even helped me with buying a house. He was a fine and decent man. It is a wonder how people differ from one person to another.

Grandson, Bahador

"Recite, in the name of thy Lord who createth man from a clot, & thy Lord is the most Bounteous, who teacheth by the pen, that which he knew not...,"

~ *H. Quran*

"Mon enfant! I give you my love, more precious than money, I give you myself...,"

~ *Walt Whitman*

Setareh called me one day to tell me that she was pregnant. The news was most electrifying. I was immersed in joy. In the months that followed, I basked in the sweet thoughts of her impending delivery of a grandchild. And when she gave birth to my grandson, a new light in my life was kindled.

It was not my first time as a grandmother, though. I already had two grandsons by my son, Arash. They would grow up to be successful in life. But unfortunately, I did not get to spend as much time with them while growing up as I would with Setareh's son, Bahador.

Bahador was just seven months old when we noticed he had difficulty breathing at night. We had him seen by a pediatrician and were told he had to undergo a tonsillectomy. Although a surgery would have been difficult at his age, he underwent one successfully. He thankfully recovered quickly and the problem was solved.

On a related thought, I feel fortunate and am proud to have Mark as my son-in-law. He is a man of high character, integrity, and impeccable education. He is endowed with a vast knowledge of world affairs. He even knows more about Iran's history than we do!

A grandchild is uniquely dear, doubly dear in fact, because a dear one brings another dear one into this world.

As a child, Bahador confided in me with any issues he had. For instance, he would ask me to mend his toys. He would ask me to stitch his favorite clothes. When in elementary school, he was tasked with an assignment to identify and elaborate on "The Hero in Your Life." He prepared a wide presentation board with my name and picture on top and snapshots of all the things I had done for him!

***

"...a tree is judged by the fruit it bears...,"

~ Luke

Mark believed that their son should learn his mother tongue as well as his father tongue. Therefore, they early on enrolled him in a kindergarten, where Farsi was taught. But as the years passed by, subsequent schooling in English would overshadow his knowledge of Farsi.

He has, thus far, earned a bachelor's degree in economics from the reputable Emory University in Atlanta, and a master's degree in economics also, from the renowned Georgia Institute of Technology. He can still understand Farsi, though once spoken to in Farsi, he usually responds in English. When he was a toddler, barely able to utter words, I had taught him to call out his mother in Farsi whenever we lost her in a mall or a large department store,

"Mommy, *kojaiee*?" ("Where are you?")

"Mommy, kojaiee?"

And upon hearing those words, Setareh would promptly join us out of nowhere!

My adoration for my grandson is beyond words. He continues to enliven my life by calling me *Maman Joon* (dear Ma). He has recently moved to California, and I miss him dearly. But he keeps in touch with me regularly, boosting my morale every time he calls.

At this point other reminiscences come to my mind.

One is my involvement in civil activities. Even with the expansive family that I had, I still managed to socialize with the other expats in the Iranian community. I became an active member of the Persian Cultural Center of Atlanta, referred to as kanoon.

I also continued working various jobs in between my ventures but was not wholly satisfied until I thought of trying my hand at real estate. I had to study and pass a grueling exam before I could obtain a state-certified real estate license. Although a difficult undertaking awaited me, as always, I was determined to achieve my goals. Attending those real estate classes daily and preparing for the difficult exam was an uphill battle, but I persevered and did not give up.

Amid the studying, I learned some lifelong lessons too that have stayed with me for the rest of my life. For instance, I learned to say,

"I don't know."

When we do not know something, especially in our Iranian culture, we rarely acknowledge it. It is as if expressing our "not knowing" something is belittling. There, in class, I learned from my instructor to, when I do not know something, muster the courage and bring myself to simply say,

"I don't know."

In those classes, I came to realize that pretending to know it all is in direct opposition to the top two qualities needed to be successful: being self-aware and coachable. I learned that organizations encouraging and nurturing those two qualities tend to be strong, innovative, and profitable. Self-awareness and the propensity to learn are especially vital in a business environment that requires timely adaptability.

In due time, I passed the exam and became a state licensed real estate agent. It has been satisfying for me to mobilize my faculties to attain the goals I set for myself in life, although far reaching at times. And this was another such goal that I aimed at and was able to achieve. After I obtained my license, I began buying and selling properties for friends and strangers.

I successfully dealt in both residential and commercial real estate. I bought a shopping center for a client. I also helped purchase the Persian Cultural Center in the Atlanta area.

Since I knew plenty of people who travelled often, another goal I had was to obtain a license as a travel agent. I attended classes online, passed the examination, and realized that goal as well. After I obtained that license, I began to make travel accommodations for a horde of friends and relatives, including vacation cruises. My grandson Bahador still reminds me of a marvelous time he had on the Carnival Cruise I booked for him and his parents back in 2011.

Aside from my faith, I believe my optimism and sanguine demeanor have been the driving forces behind my exertions in life, catapulting me to reach new heights.

Death Comes for Shahrokh

"O Living always, always dying! O the burials of me, past & present!"

~ W. Whitman

"This is Love: to fly heavenward, to rend, every instant, a hundred veils. The first moment, to renounce Life...,"

~ Rumi

My ex-husband Shahrokh, who had been living in Gadsden Alabama, near his nephew, fell ill and was bed stricken. My daughter, Setareh, visited him weekly. My son, Arash, would also join her at times. Shahrokh, who lacked an adequate command of the English language, needed someone to talk to his doctor regarding his illness, treatments he received, and the medicines he was prescribed.

I was worried about Setareh's safety on the road each time she took that long trip from Atlanta to Gadsden. She was also a wife and a mother and had other responsibilities. I sometimes accompanied her when visiting Shahrokh, for he was still the father to my children, and it was I who had divorced him. After all, through thick and thin of life, and through the good times as well as the bad times, we had lived a lifetime together.

After he was stricken with illness, he turned for the worse in demeanor. He badgered his doctor impertinently, did not listen to his advice, and refrained from taking his medicines as he was told to. He insisted he could do better than his doctor in diagnosing his illness and even suggested outlandish medical treatments that made no scientific sense. He also had no qualms hurling a barrage of insulting remarks at his doctor every time he was examined. And his doctor was fed up with his brash behavior.

Unfortunately, in due time, his uncouth behavior would also render his doctor indifferent to his condition.

His health condition continued to deteriorate to the point where he had to be confined to a wheelchair.

We were in a quandary and had to do something about him. I had a friend who headed a hospice in Atlanta. I asked her to help us in having him admitted to a nursing home in Atlanta. I was so ashamed of his unbecoming behavior that, at first, I was hesitant to divulge my relationship with him. After reviewing his medical records, my friend said with a drawn face and a sigh,

"Wow. This patient's behavior is abhorrent, but I'll do all I can to help."

After my friend informed us that she had made a transfer possible, I left the rest to Setareh, who with resilience had her father admitted to a nursing home in Atlanta. I breathed a sigh of relief when Setareh no longer had to make those long trips to visit her father in Alabama.

But after he was finally transferred to that nursing home, he did not cease to misbehave. Again, I turned to my friend for help in transferring Shahrokh to the hospice she headed, one that was filled with the Iranians expats. She said,

"Hospices are for people near death, how can I transfer him here? But I'll try my best."

And that was also accomplished through her kind efforts. He was finally satisfied and felt comfortable among his countrymen in the new center.

Setareh and Arash visited their father a few times a week and tipped the nurses to make sure he was well taken care of. He was happy in the new surroundings because he was able to speak Farsi with the other patients, with whom he had quickly forged friendships.

He loved to play chess and backgammon—and almost always came out as a winner. In his better days, he used to teach chess to family and friends—

and that was how a lot of them remembered him by. He spent his last days playing cards, backgammon, and chess, and socializing with his new friends. That showed he was all-together and had a good command of his faculties until the very end. He passed on two years after arriving in Atlanta.

We all visited him regularly and kept a watch on him to the very end.

While we were all grief-stricken with his loss, I had a clear conscience, for I had stood by him a lifetime, enduring his misconduct. By helping him to return to America, I had given him a second chance in the hope of living a tranquil life. I know I must have been one of the rare and few Iranian women who had divorced their husbands. But I should have left him sooner, at a younger age. Instead, I stuck it out with him mostly for the sake of my children. I tried hard to pull my family together, wishing for the best, which did not exactly materialize.

Unfortunately, our gracious friend at the hospice, whose memory is always with us, also died, of a surgery gone wrong.

September 11, 2001

"I never saw the heavens so dim by day...a savage clamor...,"

~ Shakespeare

I must talk about a most horrifying incident that happened during my stint in the real estate realm, a terrible event that would have an everlasting impact on our world.

On a seemingly perfect day with the garish sun shining and the early autumn breeze caressing my face, I stepped out of my car and walked to the offices of Keller Williams Realty, where I was working as a real estate agent. I noticed the staff on foot, congregating, spellbound, and staring at a television screen that was showing two passenger planes diving into the Twin Towers in New York City and the explosions following the deadly collisions and the ensuing chaos.

It was a very sad day for all of us. It was a day of terror, destruction, and death. It was heart-wrenching to think of all those innocent people who had fallen victim to a group of demonic fanatics. The magnitude of that calamity was incomprehensible. Thinking of all those killed and all the families who had been affected as a result, losing loved ones, was distressing. That tragic event would leave its indelible imprint on our world in ways that no one would have thought before.

As a Muslim, I felt particularly affected by this catastrophe, because the terrorists were also Muslims. But I was convinced that my faith had nothing in common with theirs. My Islam is rooted in worshipping a benevolent God, a loving God, whose revealed scriptures say that if you kill one man, it is as if you have killed all of humanity. I am baffled by how those who commit those atrocities can even call themselves Muslims. I believe they are no more than misguided and deranged individuals in need of psychiatric help.

For days afterwards, I could not but think of all those who had lost a father, a mother, a son, or a daughter–all the families who were forever shattered–all the lovers who would never see each other again–and all those brave first responders and firefighters who had risked their lives to save lives.

Soon, learning about Islam had become more commonplace due to a widespread desire by Americans to learn more about a religion that they thought had been the driving force behind that horrific incident.

I read somewhere that after a firefighter had read parts of the Quran, he had been so inspired by the Surah 5, Ma'idah, Ayat 32, wherein it is said, "...whoever kills a soul, is as though he had killed all mankind, and whoever saves a life, it is as though he had saved all mankind...," that he had gone, more determined than before, into the debris to help save a life.

That dreadful day too passed, but was never forgotten, and will forever "live in infamy," changing our world as we knew it.

A few years later, my activities in the real estate business began to dwindle. There simply were too many agents flooding the real estate market, whom I had to compete with. And I stood at a disadvantage with my foreign background.

Most people, especially those who had already bought real estate, already knew an agent that they preferred to work with, so they eschewed new relationships.

This field had other disadvantages too. For one, it was a time-consuming profession. Customers demanded to see many properties before making a decision. And oftentimes, after they had chosen a property, either the bank loan was not granted, or they would end up changing their minds. Of course, they have since added a paragraph to the real estate contracts that potential buyers must show proof of funding prior to engaging an agent. This was intended to save the agents from wasting their time on those who lacked the funds to purchase properties.

I continued to believe that with hard work, I could still make it in that business, but since I saw a decline in my activities, and considering my advanced age, I decided to try another venture that could financially seal and secure my retirement.

Eighth Venture - Quick Service Franchise

*"Be not discouraged...keep on...there are divine
things, well envelop'd...more beautiful than words
can tell...,"*

~ Walt Whitman

Then time came for a last try in the business world before I could retire. In choosing a business that could help me retire, I began thinking how I had thus far started businesses from the ground up, either on my own or with one or two other partners, and how risky some of them had been. This time, I thought it might be safer to venture out into a franchise-style business that had worked before and whose corporate support I could be under, giving me a higher degree of security.

After having lived in the U.S. for some time, I could not help but notice a uniquely American phenomenon in the food and beverage industry: franchising. This concept goes back to the late 19th century when one of the first successful American franchising operations was started by an enterprising druggist named John S. Pemberton. In 1886, he had concocted a beverage, comprising sugar, molasses, spices, and cocaine. He had then licensed selected people to bottle and sell the drink, which had become what is now, minus the cocaine, known as Coca-Cola, one of the earliest and most successful franchising operations in the world. And later, a trove of other franchising ventures, fast-food chains, including the famed McDonalds, Burger King, and Kentucky Fried Chicken, had popped up, blanketing the American landscape from coast to coast.

Simply put, the lure of franchise was too tempting to resist. Wherever I went, I was bombarded by a myriad of recognizable signages of fast-food chains, reinforcing the belief that those brick-and-mortar operations were there to stay. Therefore, this time, I decided to invest in a franchise that would fit my requirements: one that had worked before, was relatively simple to operate, required a modest capital investment, and that I could operate without a background in the hospitality industry.

I particularly thought that the support offered by a franchisor coupled with brand recognition would lower the risk of failure. I reasoned that if a food concept had succeeded elsewhere, it was bound to succeed in a burgeoning market such as Atlanta. And if I was able to successfully operate a pilot store in that market, expanding to a multi-store chain would not have been far-fetched. And once I was established in the Atlanta market, I could exercise my exit strategy: to sell my chain of quick service restaurants to other newly arrived immigrants looking to own a business—and finally retire.

After taking a bird's eye's view of the franchise-market landscape, I requested information and booklets from a few sandwich-shop chains. Most of them had requirements that I could not fulfill. Some asked for a large sum of initial capital investment, which I lacked. Others required extensive experience in the hospitality industry, which I did not have either.

I finally located one franchisor by the name of New York Subs that fitted my situation. With a high-end and relatively simple menu, they offered high quality sandwiches. I could also afford the initial investment, an up-front franchise fee of $12,000, a much lower figure in comparison to what other more recognized companies required. I saw this as the opportunity I was waiting for. But more importantly, they had no branches in Atlanta that I had to compete with. I would be their entrée into this bustling retail market, giving me a sense of exclusivity, and a chance to develop the market, growing into a multi-store operation.

I contacted their offices in Arizona and proceeded with the steps I had to take. I rented a desirable location next to a Starbucks in a shopping center, thinking that I could take advantage of the crowd a Starbucks would draw. There were also many office buildings in the vicinity of that shop, making it an ideal location. "What better location than next to a Starbucks in a densely populated area, particularly office employees, to guarantee success?" I thought. My research had shown that a sandwich shop usually thrived on the pull of the lunch crowd of office employees. Between the food concept and the location, I felt I had a recipe for success. Surprisingly, the franchisor refrained from imparting an opinion regarding the location, as if it did not matter. Only after they came to install their equipment did they say,

"This is a good location."

They shifted the burden of negotiating the lease to me, claiming that since they had no footholds in Atlanta, it would be more appropriate for me to negotiate and consummate such matters.

I paid them their initial franchise fee and set off to Arizona for training. I attended their Arizona makeshift training school, not much more than an ordinary sandwich shop.

I was to be their first and last franchisee in Atlanta because they had no desire to stay in business much longer. In a way, I was to be their guinea pig in the Atlanta market. I felt it odd that they neither bothered with negotiating my lease, nor did they show any interest in voicing any opinions regarding my store's frontage sign-board that sat on the front marquee.

The franchisor was a corporation, whose shares were owned by the members of a family, including a father, wife, son, and a daughter. With the aid of a franchise attorney, they had been able to register their rights and trademarks, put a franchise package together, and become a franchisor. After registering as a lawful franchisor, they had set out to lure the public to become their franchisees, paying them the upfront franchise fees and buying their equipment and products. But they gravely failed in supporting their franchisees, and did not much care if they failed. In effect, they were only after quick money, as would later prove to be the case.

After selecting the location and signing the lease, I began the construction of the space in compliance with the standards set forth by the franchisor. I also purchased the equipment and fixtures, including refrigerators, sandwich table, signage, and other related appliances from them as they had required. Upon completion of the construction, the equipment and fixtures arrived and were installed, employees were hired, and the training got underway.

Finally, the day of the grand opening arrived. I invited some friends and relatives for free sandwiches. Everyone enjoyed their meal and lavished me with compliments. The sandwiches were high-quality and the portions were generous. A couple could split a footlong sandwich between them as a single meal. The meatball club sub was incredibly popular.

The following day, the shop opened and I started to arrive there at 7 o'clock each morning to receive the freshly baked sandwich bread that was delivered by a local bakery. I would start the day by cutting up the bread and storing it in a container to keep it from getting dry. Then I would wait with great anticipation for the arrival of my lunch customers.

Due to the lack of any advertising by the franchisor, I had to print advertising materials myself that I walked and distributed among neighboring businesses and residential apartments to draw customers.

After having paid the initial franchise fee and having made other disbursements related to the conversion of the rented space into a sandwich shop in compliance with the standards that the franchisor had imposed on me, I had practically used all of my money. Once I exhausted my financial resources, to retain a working capital, I was left with no option but to borrow on my unsecured lines of credit that I had been awarded by my banks for having been a good customer.

I was financially strained.

In the first month of operation, we continuously received compliments from our customers who were happy with both our food and service. But business was gravely lagging behind my expectations. And it even went from bad to worse. Unfortunately, no matter how hard I tried, business never picked up, and I was losing money every single day, which drained me of all the savings and bank credits I had at my disposal. I needed to reach about $1,000 in sales per day to break even, but I was not able to exceed much beyond $400 per day in sales, so I was daily losing about $600.

I thought that was how the restaurant business was: in the beginning, a new restaurant lost money, then in due time after the restaurant was well established in the neighborhood, it would gradually and steadily pick up, turning profitable. Therefore, I continued to borrow more money on my lines of credit, just to pay my expenses and stay afloat, buying time, hoping against hope. I had my employees spread even more flyers and coupons, but that did not get me far either.

While the franchisor did not provide any operational or marketing support as they were bound to under the terms of our franchise agreement, I kept on paying them the monthly royalty fee that was stipulated in our agreement.

Sadly, the business did not make it. Thereupon, I defaulted on the credit facilities I had painstakingly maintained over the years. Additionally, I lost all the money I had saved over the years. After a year of hard work, I was left with no option but to file for bankruptcy in 2006.

It is unfortunate that the free-market system prevalent in America can allow some people to concoct bogus franchises and, with no precautions, bait people into investing their money in them. It is a pity how the spirit of the law is being circumvented by some for a quick gain. And worse yet, once people lose their money to such scheming people, no laws come to their aid.

***

"...birth of awareness that all things are void...,"

~ Buddha

Although the unexpected bankruptcy struck me at an old age, rendering it almost irreparable, I still did not lose hope, nor did I lose the will to continue living in a positive vein. My faith has always bolstered and prevented me from succumbing to despondency or desperation in the face of failure. Without my abiding faith, I probably could not have withstood the pressure that this unfortunate financial failure had brought upon me.

After I filed for bankruptcy, I hauled all the restaurant equipment and supplies to my garage at home. And later, someone under the direction of a court-appointed trustee purchased, for a nominal price, all that equipment still in mint condition. I wished the buyer all the best in his endeavor.

I had fallen victim to a profiteering family, who sometime later changed their franchise name and began operating under a different guise. I consulted with several attorneys, weighing the prospects of taking legal action against them, but due to the lack of financial resources, I was not able to muster the retainer sum the attorneys I consulted with required of me. There were also no guarantees for success in such a lawsuit, I was told. I had neither the money to file a complaint nor much hope for success.

I had lost everything, but I was still alive, and immersed in a piercing urge to move on with my life. By that time, in all, I had tried a total of ten different businesses in America.

In hindsight, if I ever wanted to venture out again, I would go back to the dry-cleaning business. I am well acquainted with it and could manage multiple stores without even working in them on a day-to-day basis. But unfortunately, at my age, I am at a disadvantage to try another business yet again.

Sister, Firoozeh

"...it was the age of wisdom, it was the age of foolishness, it was the epoch of belief, it was the epoch of incredulity, it was the season of light, it was the season of darkness, it was the spring of hope, it was the winter of despair...,"

~ Charles Dickens

After some 20 years of seemingly happy married life, my sister Firoozeh and her husband were faced with certain irreconcilable differences that sadly resulted in their separation. This came as a hard blow to not only her, but to the rest of the family as well. From all appearances, their family life with two wonderful children to the end seemed nothing but full of love. Friends used to tease them, saying they were on a perennial honeymoon.

Firoozeh was also a great mother to her two children. I recall that when she enrolled her children in preschool, she applied for a job there, just to be with them. That continued until they entered elementary school.

Nonetheless, her marriage crashed into a divorce. And she subsequently remarried in about a year, this time to an American fellow who expressed amorous sentiments toward her. Firoozeh mistook those sentiments to be genuine and consented to marry him. But those romantic words would later prove to be untrue.

Their wedding, quite different from any other, was held on a memorable night on a yacht at Lake Lanier, a popular destination in northern Georgia, with relatives from all over in attendance. The yacht anchored off at a pristine location for the formal wedding ceremony, and after the ceremony, off to sea, it sailed again for many unforgettable hours of music and dancing.

The bride shone in a white short dress, and with an ever-immaculate hairdo, adorned with a white magnolia, she looked much like a fashion model out of *Vogue*.

She had early on been trained as a licensed hairstylist when we first came to America. After she gained adequate experience in that trade, she opened a salon of her own. Her hard work and expertise paid off, and she built up a loyal number of clienteles. And later, once she remarried and felt financially more secure, she opened a second salon.

During the time that I was not working and had ample free time, she asked me to help and manage her second salon, and I accepted. I did so not only to help my sister, whom I loved and cared for, but also because I needed to work. It was a win-win situation for the two of us. Our bond had been beyond sisterhood. Since she was much younger than me, I loved her more like my own daughter Setareh, and had taken her under my wings from a young age.

At her request, I sprang to action and started managing her second salon. I tended to general managerial duties, such as keeping track of and recording sales and controlling and disbursing the customary business expenses, including rent, utilities, and the payroll.

Firoozeh's husband occasionally barged in, pretending to check on things, but it was clear that he disliked my presence there, managing the salon. His animosity for me grew and went so far as him colluding with the other employees against me. He resented my strict management style, particularly when it came to guarding the proceeds. He did not like that I had left no room for him or anyone else to take out cash from the till. He only saw in my leaving an opportunity for indulging in impropriety. Henceforth, he did not cease to stoke the fire of dissent against me by the rest of the crew.

He also began to influence my sister, asking her to discharge me. He finally succeeded. Having constantly been complained to prompted Firoozeh to cave in to his wishes and ask me to leave. She mistakenly thought no one but her husband was best protecting her interests.

Not much time passed after my departure before Firoozeh's husband revealed his true self, too.

Once I was gone, with no one left to control the money, he had been at liberty to regularly empty the till of all the proceeds, and since the bank account was consistently short of money, he was not able to pay the rent for months. One day, Firoozeh had received a legal notice from the property owner, threatening to sue her for past due rentals. Only then did she realize that as a result of her husband's flagrant improprieties, she had been taken advantage of and that the business had accrued much debt, teetering on the edge of insolvency.

She ended up closing down the salon, and ended her marriage as well.

To this day, she continues to operate her first salon with great success. She also generously gives me free service when it comes to my hair, including cutting, dying, and styling, and does not hesitate to give me advice regarding shampoos that best suit my hair—for which I am always grateful!

Nephew, Fardad

"One generation passeth away & another generation cometh, but the earth abideth forever...,"

~ Ecclesiastes

"I gazed into my own heart; there I saw Him; he was nowhere else...,"

~ Rumi

As I am about to bring my remembrances to a close, I cannot help but recall my beloved nephew's wedding in Iran. During the 40 years that I have lived in America, I have visited my home country only four times. One of those trips was made to attend the wedding of my nephew, Fardad. My memory of that trip, however, is a bittersweet one!

Fardad is a kind, caring, and responsible member of the family. I am particularly fond of him. Our relationship is uniquely warm. He had tirelessly helped me with my financial affairs, including my retirement allowances in Iran–a task far from easy–and for which I am forever grateful to him.

I was overflowing with joy when I heard the news of his upcoming wedding and could not wait to take part in the ceremonies. The rest of the family and I, who lived in the United States, months in advance started buying wedding gifts, which were essentially jewelry items. And I was designated to represent them at the wedding.

I got ready for my long journey. As a dual national, I had both my passports renewed. I tucked them securely away alongside the wedding presents and some cash in my handbag that I usually tightly kept around my shoulder. Next, I had to board the plane and travel halfway across the globe. It suddenly struck me how my compatriots can make such an arduous journey year-round.

I had planned to, after arriving in Tehran, catch a connecting flight to Shiraz, where my sister Parvaneh has continued to live. From there we planned to, together with her and her family, fly to Tehran to attend the much-anticipated wedding ceremonies.

Finally, I arrived in Shiraz, although, disoriented and in a daze due to the long flight.

The day following my arrival in Shiraz, we all decided to visit the tomb of Hafez, the famous Iranian poet and mystic located in Shiraz, and for whom the city is famous. I left the house with the same handbag over my shoulder, oblivious to all the jewelry, cash, and my passport I was carrying in it. As we stepped out of the car, a beggar in rags approached me, pleading for money. I pulled out a dollar bill from my handbag and gave it to him. He showered me with a long, inquisitive look and did not say anything, but kept a vigilant eye on me.

As we were strolling along, enjoying the pleasant air, we fell deep into a conversation about spirituality, religion, and prayer. My brother-in-law kept questioning me teasingly, as he always did. For instance, he brought up the subject of women wearing a veil when praying (that I am against), and I was responding, quoting chapter and verse from the Holy Scriptures: "no one is closer to us humans as the loving God who created us from a drop of sperm." Islam asserts that our maker is closer to us than the jugular vein in our necks, carrying blood to our vital organs. God is omnipotent and omnipresent, including beneath the veil. He is all knowing. And he is unbiased toward gender. If men can pay their daily devotions without a veil, why can't women?

He then began to challenge and criticize my puritan faith which disregards the man-made additions to the original Islam, and has only the Quran as its core. Hence, a passionate religious conversation got underway.

My sister and her husband are, nonetheless, pious Muslims and regularly read the Holy Book. But they read it in Arabic, which is not their mother tongue. Therefore, I believe they cannot comprehend it as they should. The Holy Book, specifically, urges the believers to read it in their mother tongues for better comprehension. This, my brother-in-law insisted, was going against orthodoxy and not acceptable. My way of practicing Islam, he said, was concocted.

We continued to leisurely saunter on the wide sidewalk that stretched out from the tomb of Hafez, deep in conversation, when all of a sudden, out of nowhere, a motorcycle with two youngsters on it sped toward me. One of them reached for my handbag, snatching it, and dragging me along with it on the asphalt as they whizzed by. My handbag had entangled around my arm and could not be separated from me, so they had to let go and flee. I was shocked and frightened to the bone and could not bring myself to fathom what had just happened. It all happened so fast that my mind could not grasp it all in time. My knees were badly scraped. My teeth had hit the ground, and blood was gushing out of my mouth. My eyeglasses were nowhere to be found. All I could think was,

"What would have I done, had they taken my handbag with all the jewelry I had brought for Fardad and his new bride, and my passport, and my cash, and...?

The miraculous way I survived this incident, without seriously getting hurt or losing anything, was thought-provoking. I kept on asking myself: how could these two people, who were most likely experienced muggers, fail to steal my bag?

I believe Godly love, in coordinating and unfolding of events, is busy doing its work, here and now...

That incident among a few others I have experienced during my lifetime, was further proof that miracles do happen. I believe being spiritually committed to and in sync with the providence has such consequences that our cerebral faculties cannot fathom.

***

"The Lord is my shepherd...,"
~ Psalm

In the days that followed, after I recounted the story of that incident to others, I heard frightful tales of victims of similar muggings, who had ended up with severed arms, broken legs, and injured heads. I was told that I was very fortunate for having survived the attempted mugging unscathed. Again, I credit my faith, and have trust in my maker for being my protector and being there for me in time of need.

We flew to Tehran the next day. Since the government had banned Western style celebrations that hosted unveiled women alongside men, it was decided that the wedding reception, surreptitiously, take place at the groom's house. The government agents were notorious for barging in, breaking up, and even arresting the attendees if they knew a ceremony was being held without strict adherence to the Islamic dress codes and laws.

The wedding, then, had to take place at my brother's verdant garden, which was the backyard of a luxurious high-rise apartment building that he had constructed.

I found that particular wedding ceremony and the reception that followed the following day in Iran to be unique. The ceremony was exceedingly detailed and elaborate. The reception featured an abundance of eats, unmatched by anything I had seen before. The service was excellent. And the music was immaculate.

Trays upon trays, piled up with colorful seasonal fruits and fine confectionaries, were set in unique claw-feet silver trays, atop the multitude of round tables. Men in uniform, roaming nonstop, passed refreshments on silver trays. The dinner buffet featured a myriad of traditional Iranian and continental savory dishes that could please any taste.

Men dressed in designer suits and women in the latest haute contours were mingling animatedly. The air was filled with the smell of what seemed to be a mixture of all the perfumes and the colognes that the French had ever invented.

The moon had risen high among the many stars as if taking part in the celebrations. The air vibrated with chatter. Hilarity increased by the minute. And roaring laughter rose to the clear sky on that balmy summer night.

With the arrival of the newlyweds, the air thundered with cheers. They were showered with mint bills as they walked through the crowd. And kids hurried to pick up the fallen bills.

The live band played with zest and all tried their newest dancing moves with zeal.

And the rounds of refreshments kept coming. And the music roared higher.

The official wedlock ceremony administered, in the Islamic tradition, had taken place at my brother's home the day before the reception. There, a beautifully arranged sofreh aghd, adorned with the two towering wedding candelabras and a mirror, lush flowers, and other customary items was the center of attraction.

As mentioned before, in keeping with the Iranian traditions, the sofreh aghd is displayed before the groom and the bride when legal marriage is performed by an officiant and nuptial vows are exchanged. These traditional practices date back thousands of years to when Zoroastrianism was the official religion of the Iranians. Today, since Iranians have diverse religious backgrounds, the sofreh aghd has more of a cultural significance, and not of faith. The word sofreh means spread and aghd means the marriage ceremony. The items displayed on the spread are primarily symbolic. They represent elements portending a happy married life for the couple.

Those items include,

Mirror: a mirror facing the couple represents light radiating into marriage. Traditionally the couple take one look into the mirror together.

Candelabras: a pair of candelabras symbolizes energy in the couple's life together.

Flatbread: a decorative display of flatbread with a heart graffiti on it symbolizes feasts to be spread in the married life. Additionally, feta cheese and fresh herbs are rolled into this type of flatbread, cut-up to bite size, and served to the guests as finger food.

Fruits: usually pomegranates and apples are used to represent a joyous future.

Rock Candy: a bowl is over-filled with whole rock candy branches, sticking out, symbolizing a sweet life for the newlyweds.

Gold Coins: they represent wealth and financial prosperity for the couple. They are poured over the couple's heads at the closure of the wedding ceremony.

Honey: at the end of the ceremonial recitations by the officiate, the couple dip their pinkies in the honey and, locking arms, feed each other, representing everlasting sweet relationship between the two.

Rose water: it was used to perfume the air in the old days. It is also poured on the fingers of the couple from a silver pitcher over a silver basin after the honey dipping act.

Quran: is set on the spread, invoking God's blessing for the marriage. The Holy Book is usually opened from the middle and placed in front of the couple as a symbol of faith.

Sweets and Pastries: an assortment of traditional baked sweets and pastries are displayed on silver trays to be shared with the guests after the formal wedding ceremony is concluded, symbolizing sharing the sweetness of life with family and friends.

Sugar Cloth: it is a white, fine fabric held over the couple throughout the ceremony by various happily married female relatives and friends, each taking turn in holding a corner.

Sugar Cones: happily married female relatives or friends take turn in rubbing the sugar cones together over the Sugar Cloth that is held over the couple, showering their marriage and lives with everlasting sweetness.

Wild Rue: this is an herb which is burned to purify, and to rid the couple of negative energy.

Traditional Embroidered Cloth: an expensive decorative traditional embroidered cloth named *Termeh*, handed down from generations past, symbolizes family and tradition.

A hush fell with the utterance of wedding rites and the exchange of wedding vows. The bride's consent was asked and, as it is the custom, she did not give her consent on the first request, but uttered it on the third. The groom imparted his consent on the first query as he was supposed to.

After the wedding was officiated and the marriage certificate was signed by the couple, relatives, and friends stood in line to kiss the newlyweds and shower them with jewelry and gold coins.

Then came time for taking pictures with the couple in groups that lasted a long time.

The bride looked wonderful in her glitzy wedding gown. And I was thrilled to give them my gifts, without which I would have been miserably embarrassed. Fardad is akin to a son for me, and his beautiful bride is like a daughter.

Fraud in the Digital Age

"Old age, calm, expanded, broad with the haughty
breadth of the universe, old age, flowing free with
the delicious near-by freedom of death...,"

~ From 'Leaves of Grass'

Not many years ago, with the indispensable aid of the Iranian expats in Atlanta, a Persian Cultural Center, known as kanoon, was established. Despite the lack of adequate financial support, this center had been able to keep its door open to the Iranians diaspora in Atlanta.

This center, registered under the laws of the state of Georgia, has been instrumental in finding employment for those expats seeking employment. Other services offered have included family counseling, Farsi language classes, cultural events, planning festivities for Nowruz, and the hosting of notable guests, delivering speeches on a variety of social subjects and current events.

Over the years, I have remained a permanent, active member of this center and have not hesitated to do all I can to help advance its success. The management team is selected for a period of four years. I have twice served as a member of the management team. Having been a native of Shiraz, I have also twice arranged festivities dubbed "The Night of Shiraz," which have featured local cuisine, music, and speeches, signifying cultural characteristics of my beloved hometown.

My next story involves the domain of today's technology. Technology, if used properly, can undoubtedly be a blessing. But more often than not, it is used in a diabolic vein. Unfortunately, a sea of scams has seeped into this domain. These include everything from defrauding elderlies to hacking major industries to interfering with presidential elections. Sometimes I wonder if the founders of today's technology could ever foresee such mischiefs, and if so, would they have still gone through with their inventions?

In 1990, I read an article in the New York Times about a young Iranian entrepreneur by the name of Morad Omidyar, also known as Pierre, the founder of eBay. He had turned a billionaire by nurturing a new idea that had, literally, taken the market by a storm. The story went that he and his mother had been in the possession of used household items that they did not wish to keep, nor did they want to give them away. After brooding over a solution, Pierre had come up with the noble idea of advertising their unwanted items on a site that he created on the internet by the name of eBay.

The flood of people who had volunteered to purchase his unwanted items had surprised him. He had decided to expand the site he had created to include others in the same predicament as he had been, needing to sell their used belongings. And soon, people, companies, and organizations had flocked to his site to advertise, and the rest is history.

His brilliant idea had eventually made him a billionaire while at the same time it had generated much economic activity in terms of buying and selling in the market, contributing to stimulate the aggregate economy.

***

"You shall not heap up what is call'd riches, you shall scatter with lavish hand all that you earn or achieve...,"

~ Walt Whitman

After reading about him, I was impressed by what he had been able to accomplish at such a young age, so I began to develop a profound interest and a keen liking in him. I felt proud to have a countryman, who with his genius, had been able to solve a simple, collective human problem. I was already aware that the Iranian expats in America, as key players of some of the most iconic organizations, such as Google, Yahoo, Instagram, and even NASA, had been successful in innovations.

I was particularly impressed with Pierre's philanthropic approach in life. He and his mother, I read, were major contributors to Iranian causes also. I had also read on a site that he had said he only spent 10% of his income for his personal use. The rest, he had claimed he donated to the needy and worthy causes. It occurred to me that he might even be interested in helping us in Atlanta to secure a more suitable physical location for the new kanoon center we had recently established.

I continued to be enamored by Pierre as a mother would be of her son and continued to follow him in that vein online. I liked the fact that not only had he made a fortune for himself, but he had created numerous jobs and provided massive economic opportunities for the general public.

I avariciously read any article I could find on him. I soon knew which charitable organizations he had contributed to, how many offices he had, how many houses he owned and where, which notable persons worked for him, etc. I was so taken by the success of this young man that I, unknowingly, fell victim to the scheme of an imposter who presented himself as Pierre. I had, at first hand, crossed paths with dishonest people, but I did not expect to find rogue schemers in the digital domain as well.

I had thought Facebook to be a safe and secure site, so one day, I searched his name and dropped an account named "Pierre Omidyar" a note on Facebook Messenger, through which I keep in touch with a lot of people and had never experienced any foul play. He quickly responded with a warm return note, bearing his family pictures and credentials. My suspicion was aroused at first, but then I thought, this might be God's doing. I was so happy that I called Setareh immediately,

"I've found a new son. Pierre has answered me."

I would send him messages on occasions, to which he always responded promptly.

Then I began to wonder, how can someone like Pierre, with all his other duties and workload, afford to take the time out of his busy schedule to respond to my messages. He even started asking questions of me, to which I eagerly responded. One time, he went as far as extending an invitation to meet me.

"I would love to meet you in Malaysia," he suggested.

"Why? We both live in America. Why should we be meeting in Malaysia?" wrote I.

He explained,

"Well, I'll be there on business and I'll have plenty of time at my disposal in the evenings after work. I can spend time with you then. I'm impressed with your life story. I'm interested to meet such a brave person who has always braced herself in the face of hardships."

I answered,

"Me too. I'm impressed by such a young genius, whom I adore like a son."

He added,

"Whenever you decide on coming to Malaysia to meet me, please give me ample advance notice, so I can have my travel agency arrange for your ticket."

With this offer of sending me plane tickets through his own travel agency, I could not help but think that he truly was Pierre.

I could not accept his offer at that time, because my passport had expired, and later I would thank God for it. Therefore, I wrote,

"My passport has expired. It is a pity that I can't meet you in Malaysia."

Finally, one day he asked,

"What is it that I can do for you?"

I, who was an active member of the management team of the nascent Persian Cultural Center, scrambling to solve the location problem for that organization at the time, explained,

"I would like for you to buy a piece of property in your own name and allow the Persian Cultural Center in Atlanta use it in continuing their services to the Iranian community here. Your name will forever be remembered by the members of our community, as one supporting the Iranian culture."

He snapped, "Find the location."

I answered ecstatically,

"I, myself, am a real estate agent and can find a suitable building in no time."

I was happy that he had accepted to help. I went to work and after much research and looking around, I found two properties in the price ranges of 2 and 3 million dollars. I sent the files that bore all the pertinent information regarding those two properties, to the email address he had sent me:

Pierreomidyar321@usa-11.com

Since he had given me his personal email address, I no longer doubted his sincerity.

Once he received my email, he asked,

"In your opinion, which property is better?"

I responded,

"The $3 million one has a better location with more potential for future growth."

He easily accepted to purchase the property,

"It is fine with me. Please use the same email address and send me the rest of the documentation on the property."

He added,

"Also, please do send all of your personal information, including full name, passport number, bank address, account number, phone and fax numbers, etc., to the bank, below."

I was taken aback.

"The property will be purchased in your name. Why do you need my personal information?"

He reasoned,

"Well, it would be easier if you initially bought the property in your name. After the purchase takes place in your name, I'll fly down to transfer the title to my name. I need your personal information so I can have my bank wire you the money."

I tried to explain,

"Well. This is not the way to purchase a property. You need to hire a local attorney and the money needs to be retained in his escrow account until such time as the sale is finalized."

He said assuring,

"I trust you."

How could someone send that much money to some stranger? I thought.

Subsequently, I received an email from a bank by the name of, UK Charter Bank, bearing a bank letterhead with such information as, a location address, a phone, and a fax number (e-bankinaccount@scbmy.com...fax 011 44 7543189397).

"This is pursuant to a request by our special customer, Mr. Omidyar. We have been advised of a pending real-estate transaction. To avoid any unexpected contingencies, we are duty-bound to have all of your personal information on our records. Therefore, kindly provide the same to us at the address above."

After observing the bank officer's signature affixed to his name, I felt assured that all was authentic and I was doing a great favor for the Iranian community in Atlanta.

I forwarded him all of my personal information. A few days later, the same bank officer followed up with a phone call, introducing himself, and spoke at length on the importance of his customer, Mr. Omidyar, asking me to provide him with the best service possible. Afterwards, I received a follow-up email from him,

"To proceed with the purchase of the property located at...on behalf of Mr. Omidyar, please deposit the sum of $4,300 in his account number,"

This was the defining moment when suspicion finally reared its head and I decided to consult with my own bank, recounting all that had transpired thus far.

They warned me,

"This is known as a 'senior scam'. It's a fraud."

***

> "Wolves which batten upon lambs, lambs consumed
> by wolves, there you have nature...,"
>
> ~ Marquis de Sade

Whoever the trickster was, in the end, his trick did not work. But I felt downcast and forlorn for having had all my sanguine hopes dashed, and precious time wasted. I was also upset at myself for having been overly naïve and trusting.

After this heart-wrenching, anticlimactic fiasco that lasted some five months and played with my nerves, I began to worry for the real Omidyar, whose name had been the subject of such a diabolical scheme. I wrote a long letter to him, explaining in detail the saga I had been through, hoping to give him heads up so that he could prevent such schemes from happening in the future in his good name. I sent copies of the letter to his offices in California and New York, as well as his home address. I further called his offices, narrating the event in detail. I even wrote his mother a heartfelt letter, informing her of the fraud that was taking place in his son's name.

I received no replies.

When reflecting on my past, I sometimes wonder at all the ups and downs that a life begets. Life is full of little moments, significant as well as insignificant, that compound to form a life. It is filled with stories, good and bad.

Once you uproot yourself and choose to grow roots in a different land, life's calculus changes dramatically. You will have to set aside a good part of your old mode of existence and adopt new ones. It is you who must assimilate. Much like a newborn, you have to start anew. Aside from the new language, you must learn the new laws, the new customs, and the new human exchanges.

But I am still grateful that at my age, despite all the setbacks and failures I have endured, I continue to live a happy and active life independent of others. And I feel blessed to have been endowed with such positive energy that I yearn to share with others.

And today I am content to continue making a living, this time, on the Internet.

And like the legendary French singer Edith Piaf says, *"Je ne regrette rien* ("I have no regrets")."

Epilogue

"Remember, remember always that all of us, and you and I especially, are descended from immigrants and revolutionists...,"

~ *Franklin D. Roosevelt*

When on board the plane heading to the land of opportunities, I thought of all those who before me had embarked on that same journey. I thought of the 102 pilgrims who fled religious persecution in England and risked their lives, setting sail on the Mayflower to reach America some four centuries ago.

Those were the same brave men and women who established the Plymouth Colony in Massachusetts. A colony that grew out of only a few courageous migrants, half of whom later perished due to illness caught on the sea. And thus, they gave their lives for freedom and democracy. They gave their lives, so that countless other migrants like me could follow in their footsteps and reap the benefits of a free democratic country. They did not die in vain.

And so, the migration continued. And they sailed westward against all odds, into the future, so they could live in the land of the free.

However, attitudes toward new immigrants by those who came before have vacillated between welcoming and not so welcoming over the years. And when it was us Iranians emigrating in 1978, the welcoming sentiments were certainly lacking.

Relations between Iranians and American had begun in the middle of the 19th century. Iranians, wary of the British and Russian colonial interests, had considered America as a friendly nation. Many American missionaries had been dispatched to Iran, and they were well received.

Iranians participating in the constitutional revolution, fighting to break free of British and Russian meddling in Iranian affairs, had always viewed the U.S. as sympathetic to Iran's quest for independence and democracy. The Americans were considered as the good guys, who had no colonial ambitions regarding Iran.

In the 1970s, some 25,000 American technicians were working in Iran on modernization projects. By the end of 1970s, it has been said that nearly a million Americans had visited or lived and worked in Iran, and had often expressed their admiration for the Iranian people, their culture, and their hospitality.

Having firsthand witnessed the amity between the two peoples when I lived in Iran, it still remains an unanswered question for me that, "why, when I set foot in America in 1978, I faced so much prejudice and animosity towards Iranians?" Even the amount of investment required for the Investor Visa had doubled that year, just to make it harder for Iranians to immigrate to America.

If anything, considering the warm hospitality with which the Americans had been received in Iran over the years, I had expected a similar reception in America, but it was sadly lacking.

I have come to learn that immigrants over the years have played an increasingly important role in the U.S economy because they have been more likely to start and own businesses than the U.S.-born population. After doing some research, I realized that immigrant entrepreneurs have made up more than half of the business owners in some of the "Main Street" business subcategories. "Main Street" businesses are usually broken into,

Retail: Businesses such as florists, gas stations and small grocery stores

Accommodation and Food Services: chain quick service restaurants, motels

Neighborhood Services: Businesses such as barbers, dry cleaners

These businesses have often been the seeds of economic development in localities across the U.S., creating millions of jobs and generating billions of dollars in revenues.

With the advent of technology, immigrants have been able to leave their mark in that sector as well. I read that more than 40% of companies on the U.S. Fortune 500 list were founded by immigrants or children of immigrants. Apple, the first company in the world to reach a $1 trillion valuation, was founded by Steve Jobs, the child of a Syrian immigrant. Google was co-founded by a Russian-born refugee, Sergey Brin. eBay was founded by an Iranian immigrant, Morad Omidyar.

Entrepreneurs starting new ventures share common experiences with immigrants embarking on a new life in a different country. The qualities that help immigrants adapt to their adopted homelands mirror those that help entrepreneurs succeed: a frontier spirit, a strong dose of grit and a unique perspective on gaps in the market. Successful businesses are those which continually adapt to the world's changing environment. Similarly, immigrants usually have an adaptable attitude as they leave their homes to travel to their adopted country. In the new settings, immigrants learn to adapt to a new culture, new market, and new laws—and adaptability, that unique quality and a key ingredient in the business world, can spill over to the realm of entrepreneurship.

After making the cumbersome journey to the U.S. and navigating the new landscape, most immigrants develop the resilience necessary to weather the obstacle-ridden road of entrepreneurship, where an indomitable spirit is also a prerequisite for success. They often develop the courage to pick themselves up after each failure and try again. And that is some of the stuff that the spirit of entrepreneurship is made of.

In a nutshell, for those who have come here on a one-way ticket to a new home, starting or owning a business has been a great benefit not only for themselves and their families but also for their adopted country. And by embracing the diverse contributions of these robust immigrants, America has been able to tap into a unique entrepreneurial spirit that has made it the greatest country on Earth.

And so, I never gave up, continued my journey, and yet again ventured out.

This time, into writing my own story.

<u>Last Word</u>

I know not
Me standing here is my fate or fault
But counting my gain or loss
Since I found God
No matter what the loss
I now know the saga of life is not, but God's lover's play with us

The End...

Farah Farnia

"Every end is a new beginning..."

Map of Iran (Places I Lived)

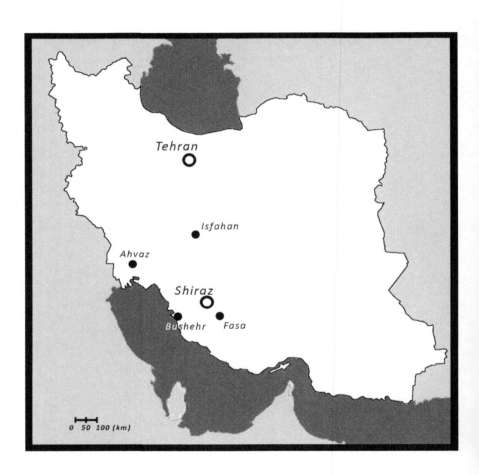

Printed in Great Britain
by Amazon